*Julie H...* (handwritten) S0-ARO-327

# Healing A
# Broken Heart

## 12 Steps of Recovery for Adult Children

by Kathleen W.

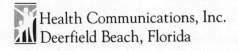
Health Communications, Inc.
Deerfield Beach, Florida

Kathleen W.
Eureka, California

**Library of Congress Cataloging-in-Publication Data**

W., Kathleen, 1941-
    Healing a broken heart.

    At head of title: Adult Children of Alcoholics.
    1. Co-dependence (psychology)   2. Adult children
of alcoholics.   3. Alcoholics Anonymous.   I. Adult
Children of Alcoholics (Organization)   II. Title.
RC569.5.C63W14   1988   362.2'9286   87-32527
ISBN 0-932194-65-6

©1988 Health Communications, Inc.

ISBN 0-932194-65-6

All rights reserved. Printed in the United States of America. No part of this
publication may be reproduced, stored in a retrieval system or transmitted in any
form or by any means, electronic, mechanical, photocopying, recording or
otherwise without the written permission of the publisher.

Published by Health Communications, Inc.
        Enterprise Center
        3201 Southwest 15th Street
        Deerfield Beach, FL 33442

*Cover Design by Reta Kaufman*

# CONTENTS

# FOREWORD

Writing through the Steps this way as I have in making this book has been a wonderful experience. I hope you will enjoy reading it, that your thinking and imagination will be stimulated. I hope some of you will form step-writing groups of your own, sharing in this kind of process directly.

The format of this book for each of the twelve steps is to suppose that you are being asked to chair a meeting on Step 10 next week. What would you say to open up discussion?

Each of these steps has been given more consideration than a 10-minute opening statement at a discussion meeting. Each of them seems to warrant two or three meetings, instead of one. If this book is being used as the focus of a "study group" meeting, I suggest you consider breaking each of the steps up into smaller units, dividing them wherever it seems comfortable to your group.

In addition to my writing group, who have continued to support me in this effort, I would also like to thank some special people who have contributed to this work through the tools and love they have provided to me, over the years: Dorothy D. and Dr. Elisabeth B.-R. of the Santa Cruz Religious Science Church; Gale and Irene Y. of the Ukiah, California A.A./Al-Anon fellowship; my sponsors these past nine years and to the memory of Charlie B., one of the founders of A.A. who I was fortunate to share some 24 hours with for the first few years of my recovery. I also wish to thank my husband, Jim W., whose combination of pepper-and-patience remains an incentive in my life for growth. Also my deepest thanks to all of you *anonymous friends* who loved and welcomed me when I couldn't love myself!

# THE PROBLEM

Many of us found that we had several characteristics in common as a result of being brought up in an alcoholic household.

We had come to feel isolated, uneasy with other people, especially authority figures.

To protect ourselves, we became people-pleasers, even though we lost our own identities in the process. All the same, we would mistake any personal criticism as a threat.

We either became alcoholics ourselves or married them or both. Failing that, we found another compulsive personality, such as a workaholic, to fulfill our sick need for abandonment.

We lived life from the standpoint of victims. Having an overdeveloped sense of responsibility, we preferred to be concerned with others rather than ourselves. We somehow got guilt feelings when we stood up for ourselves rather than giving in to others. Thus, we became reactors rather than actors, letting others take the initiative.

We were dependent personalities — terrified of abandonment — willing to do almost anything to hold onto a relationship in order not to be abandoned emotionally. Yet we kept choosing insecure relationships because they matched our childhood relationship with alcoholic parents.

These symptoms of the family disease of alcoholism made us "co-victims" — those who take on the characteristics of the disease without necessarily ever taking a drink. We learned to keep our feelings down as children and kept them buried as adults. As a result of this conditioning, we confused love with pity, tending to love those we would rescue. Even more self-defeating, we became addicted to excitement in all our affairs, preferring constant upset to workable relationships.

This is a description, not an indictment.

(Used with the permission of Adult Children of Alcoholics Central Service Board, P.O. Box 35623, Los Angeles, California 90035.)

# THE SOLUTION

The Solution is to become your own loving parent.

As the ACoA group becomes a safe place for you, you will find the freedom to express all the hurts and fears you have kept inside and to free yourself from the shame and blame that are carry-overs from the past. You will become an adult who is imprisoned no longer by childhood reactions. You will recover the child within you, learning to accept and love yourself.

The healing begins when we risk moving out of isolation. Feelings and buried memories will return. By gradually releasing the burden of unexpressed grief, we slowly move out of the past. We learn to reparent ourselves with gentleness, humor, love and respect.

This process allows us to see our biological parents as the instruments of our existence. Our actual parent is a Higher Power whom some of us choose to call God. Although we had alcoholic parents, our Higher Power gave us the 12 Steps of Recovery.

This is the action and work that heals us; we use the Steps; we use the meetings; we use the telephone. We share our experience, strength and hope with each other. We learn to restructure our sick thinking one day at a time. When we release our parents from responsibility for our actions today, we become free to make healthful decisions as actors, not reactors. We progress from hurting to healing to helping. We awaken to a sense of wholeness we never knew was possible.

By attending these meetings on a regular basis, you will come to see parental alcoholism for what it is: a disease that infected you as a child and continues to affect you as an adult. You will learn to keep the focus on yourself in the here and now. You will take responsiblity for your own life and supply your own parenting.

You will not do this alone. Look around you and you will see others who know how you feel. We will love and encourage you, no matter what. We ask you to accept us just as we accept you.

This is a spiritual program based on action coming from love. We are sure that as the love grows inside you, you will see beautiful changes in all your relationships, especially with God, yourself and your parents.

(Used with the permission of Adult Children of Alcoholics Central Service Board, P.O. Box 35623, Los Angeles, California 90035.)

# PREFACE

Many good and useful books are out now, describing the special characteristics and problems of children of alcoholics (and other dysfunctional homes). Lack of, or loss of, personal identity or purpose, fear of abandonment or of confinement, feelings of isolation coupled with an inability to trust, usually head the list of symptoms. Compulsiveness, restlessness, hypersensitivity and the tendency to either stuff reactions or over-react, or deny, avoid or rebel, are leading characteristic behaviors.

Some symptom behavior lists go on and on, sometimes running two to three pages, refining the focus on just how we hurt, what we fear, and the ways we try to work, act or break out of what seem to those of us who identify as hopeless situations. In everyday language, we are lost and lonely people, hurt and afraid, sinking into depression and despair because we don't know what to do about it.

We grieve over heartbreaks we may not be able to remember, rooted deep in childhood, buried by layers of repression, denial, guilt and abuse. Or we may not be able to understand just why we grieve, but we find ourselves repeating patterns of abuse and heartbreak as adults, seeking partners who will play out certain parts again and again.

Is there hope? Or are we just condemned to live out these painful days — never finding the love we've yearned for all our lives?

Fortunately, there *is* hope. More and more of us are experiencing the blessing of recovery in the growing fellowship of Adult Children of Alcoholics, (ACoA), or in one of the similar fellowships, Children of Alcoholics, (CoA), Co-Dependents Anonymous, (CoDA), as the result of applying the 12 Steps to ourselves around the issues of self-concept and reparenting. We get happy. Hopeful. More secure. Calmer. Peaceful. Able to take risks and to accept success.

As a variety of new therapies and insightful books continue to emerge, resources and methods are constantly being added to the fund of "tools" available to children of alcoholics (and other dysfunctional family backgrounds). Therapists commonly refer their clients to ACoA groups for follow-up to one-on-one or group work, since the Twelve-Step Programs have excellent track-records to their credit, and they are as available as people who use them wish to make them, while remaining essentially free.

For our part, ACoA has no "official" literature, nor is it affiliated with any therapy, church or institution, but, rather, we encourage all ACoA members to use any and all tools that they may find to be personally effective and attractive for their own growth.

As members of Adult Children of Alcoholics, we have a common base and center in our reliance on the principles expressed in the Twelve-Step Program of Recovery. All who identify with "The Problem" and "The Solution" are welcome in ACoA, regardless of any other affiliations they may have as individuals. We give no advice and make no recommendations regarding any particular therapy, method or system of belief. Tolerance and open-mindedness are watchwords of our fellowship and our program.

I personally believe it is impossible *not* to recover while working the Steps and attending meetings regularly. If a person gives over 20 minutes every day for two months to working the steps, while continuing to make at least one meeting every week, it is my experience — without exception — that real change and progress will occur. This has been my experience personally and with the people I've worked closely with in ACoA.

*Add* the 12 Steps to any methods, therapies or belief system you feel comfortable with, on a daily basis for two months. It's a fair test.

Thirty years ago I was an unhappy member of a middle-class family who presented an entirely false appearance to the world. We were abusive, selfish, contemptuous of each other, while we tried to look superior to everybody else. Some family members drank, used drugs or combined the two. Others withdrew into moral inflexibility. I loved and hurt, denied both the love and the hurt, and I hated. I longed for a quick escape.

Twenty years ago I had "escaped" while I continued to deny my buried feelings. I denied myself into pneumonia, broke and sick in an eastern city slum, a "flower-child" afloat in an environment I sought out for myself, an environment where murders and muggings were commonplace events, where "California Girls" like me were a special target for rape, where I huddled behind a bunch of locks that never were secure enough, hating and fearing my fellow human beings who threatened me. People I had met had committed suicide. Heroin addiction, cruelty and violence all around me, and idealistic plans that ended, always, in collapse — these were the extremes I manifested for myself.

I tried pulling myself together in several different ways: changing environments (back to California), changing careers and associations (from peace-and-love hippies to real estate), changing relationships (from none at all to ones that didn't work or last). Nothing worked. Depression so *deep* it seemed to be my only identity *always* triumphed.

In 1974 I wrote . . .

> love won sight from you
> and you were hollow in the sun
> empty in the moon
>
> this was a place of violence once
> and so were you   were you
> stark and brilliant in the wind
> bitter in the wind

there is only peace here now
where there once was life

you will not pass again
you are yourself nearly gone
what was fire and freedom
is lost and so are you   are you

I attempted suicide myself. I couldn't function any more. I couldn't even ask for help since I had no real idea what was wrong with me. The forms for Food Stamps were too much for me — besides, I believed I didn't deserve them and would probably be refused anyway. Drinking and drugs made the depression worse. I stayed like this for over a year. Hopeless.

I finally took a drunken fellow poet to a detox on New Year's Eve, 1975. The counselor, Jim B., referred me to AA/Al-Anon, as either an early-stages alcoholic or a very sick co-dependent. There was no such thing as ACoA then. Very little had been written on the effects of alcoholism on families.

Ten years ago I was a year and a half established on the path of my own recovery, in AA, NA and Al-Anon. I no longer lived in a city and my health and spirits had already greatly improved.

I'm not sure how my present lifestyle looks today to outside people. I'm married to a lovely man who understands me (well, enough anyway!), and we have a little house with flowers, dogs, neighborhood kids. Last year I won "Best of Show" for antique roses in my county rose show. It's not so important how it looks to others, although it's pretty obviously a lot healthier and more cheery than it was. What's important is my progress, from inside, where I live and feel it. I'm a happy hopeful person most days now. I credit the Twelve-Step Programs of Recovery. They have been central in my life all these years — the only new ingredient that's made a consistent core and given form to all my days since that New Year's Eve in 1975.

My present life and personal appearance are very, very different now as a result of embracing the 12 Steps. Of course my history is one of the more extreme cases — not a "light case" of the "effects of alcoholism".

People don't have to get so sick now with all the new developments in recovery and the program of ACoA. I seem pretty normal now, though. I'm living testimony to the power of the Twelve-Step Programs in Recovery.

## God Doesn't Make Junk

"God Doesn't Make Junk!" they used to tell me when I wasn't sure about myself, back when I was new to these programs.

I *felt* like "junk" and had done since early childhood. All my family seemed *damaged,* not whole. And I had heard more than just once, how *wrong, bad* and *useless* they found me. Clearly, "God's junk".

That "junk" feeling had been there through all those "flower-child" experiences, permeating my self-concept, influencing my choices. It was in there so *deep,* new people, different places or any amount of success or material goods couldn't seem to "fix" me. Junk. Real junk.

"Keep Coming Back!" they told me at the meetings I attended. "Talk to somebody", "Work the Steps!"

"God doesn't make junk! And we will love you until you're able to love yourself," they kept repeating at countless meetings in all the 12-Step Programs.

That's what I'd like to suggest to you — if your heart aches and you don't know how to fix it, and you suspect something rooted in your childhood may be running your life without your being able to really see it — join us.

This book contains my own personal sharing on the Twelve Steps. This is one example, one approach, one ACoA's perspective on the 12-Steps of Recovery as I've been able to apply them to the issues and goals on "The Problem" and "The Solution".

Read the Steps for yourself. Read over what I have to say about them and then get in touch with your own perspective to the best of your ability. There are no "wrong ways" to work the Steps! Agree or disagree, question, get angry: Be yourself. Be honest.

You can throw this book against the wall or leave it in a bus-stop. You can cover it in cloth, write your own thoughts in the margins. *Use it*. There are no "mistakes" in recovery, just *"growing experiences"*!

Recovery isn't always easy, but it's simple: Work the Steps. Heal with us.

Love and best wishes to you,
Kathleen W.

STEP ONE

# A PERSPECTIVE

---

*1. We admitted we were powerless over the effects of alcohol and our lives had become unmanageable.*

---

I work the First Step *backwards:* first admitting some aspect or another of my life is out of control, unmanageable, and then coming to see how my history and patterning growing up in a substance-abuse family is at the root of my dilemma. Then being able to admit that my best efforts on my own have been ineffective — that *I* am powerless.

When I came to my first ACoA meeting, my marriage was on the rocks, I was having an impossible time earning enough money, and I was 30 pounds over my comfortable weight. I couldn't seem to get anywhere on any of these fronts although I had lots of skills and abilities, and I was already a highly motivated person — I wanted to get well.

During the two years before joining ACoA, I had become a certified hypnotherapist specializing in emotional clearing work and the family. I had knowledge of my alcohol/drug-abuse family history and over a period of more than 10 years of my own sobriety and abstinence from drugs, I had worked and prayed and used the process of the Steps to the best of my ability to clear these issues, along with lots of outside help and counseling. So it wasn't that I wasn't trying.

Nonetheless, despite all the work I had undertaken on myself, even with AA and Al-Anon, I still couldn't seem to keep from judging and fearing my husband. And he's the sort of guy who works hard, brings his money home and doesn't fool around. Still, I suspected him of — I knew not what. Nor could I keep from doing it, or treating him like a dangerous enemy any time he acted angry, no matter how trivial the argument might be. My husband has his faults and weaknesses like any human being, but *I* was driving him away in my fear and suspicion, *not* "solving problems", as I liked to think. I couldn't see the ACoA patterning clearly but I had a real sense that I was doing something compulsively, something I really didn't want to do, but couldn't see and, therefore, couldn't stop.

On the income-earning level, in addition to being a hypnotherapist, I am a college graduate with 15 years' experience in a business field. I had no idea why I couldn't get through an employment interview without feeling certain the prospective employer would want someone else to fill the job. Nor could I keep emotionally focused well enough to function on my own in either field. A sense of dread: depression, rage and hopelessness clung to the whole issue of money and finances. I couldn't budge and debts piled up, a little more each passing month.

My weight issue tied into my childhood patterning more obviously. Food was a substance my mother abused. She weighed around 300 pounds during much of my childhood. I had clawed, climbed and been lifted, finally, out of my other substance abuses, one by one, over the years, and had finally got free of cigarettes, using the hypnotherapy clearing process that traced the tobacco issue down to my childhood bonding to my father, a three-pack-a-day man, who had smelled just like a Lucky Strike. With the smoking gone for a year and a half, the eating issue surfaced. Visions of my mother making delicious, fragrant sauces and delicate custards — things about her in myself I love and want to keep, but not the pounds of fat. I couldn't come up with a way of eating that was *normal* — balanced, wholesome and still elegant and fun. Meanwhile, I picked up a pound or two each month, horrifying myself with the prospect of ending up 300 pounds.

Although I was able to admit to myself that these three aspects of my life were out of control, it wasn't automatic to see ACoA issues as underlying causes of my troubles. Years of habitual denial and layers of coping skills were in the way. Also I had been a member of other 12-Step programs for several years — it seemed to me I had "the program", had already worked the Steps. Besides, I had found it necessary and desirable to go beyond the usual scope of the other 12-Step Programs, adding skills, opening myself to

4

new techniques which were commonly rejected, when I had tried to share about them and my hopes for getting "cleaner" — free of cigarettes, sugar and maybe foods which trigger allergies — at meetings. I had concluded sadly that perhaps I had gone as far with 12-Step Programs as the fellowship would bear.

I went to my first ACoA meeting out of curiosity since I did know that I qualified for membership (due to the work I had already done, both in working the steps and in therapy, uncovering the roots of disorder in my family and childhood,) I also wanted to use the program for my own goals, to share my insights and ideas, using the processes I had learned and developed in other disciplines. Those are both excellent reasons I've come to see — curiosity combined with self-interest.

Without at least a slightly opened mind (curiosity), combined with a desire to get something, personally, out of the effort, I don't think my kind of person can learn or change. Doing things "selflessly" is a big part of my problem after all. Of course, I felt ashamed to admit that I might have a contribution to make to ACoA — that's part of my disorder, too — the idea that I must somehow sneak even my best efforts into this world, since the Universe (my parents) didn't want me, and/or my best is never acceptable no matter what! When my inner guides want to slip something important by my denial walls, they make me just a little curious. I'll let myself be curious, even if I won't admit another thing.

### Problem and Solution

The reading of the Problem and the Solution at ACoA struck a chord of identification for me. I saw that the fellowship is dedicated to dealing with issues such as mine: self-esteem, other-centeredness, control and crisis-creating intensity. Equally important, the commitment to go back and to reparent ourselves/each other dissolves a fear which had undermined my entire life — the fear that there was no

5

solution, that the issues and losses of the early childhood experiences were final, could not be healed or changed. It's pretty hard for a person to admit what her problem really is when she's pretty sure there's no solution for it! And that, I realized, is what I'd always felt — condemned — because of my very early helpless years. I guess I always did feel powerless, but my Number One coping skill was to deny it. In the fellowship of ACoA, I was encouraged to admit my powerlessness.

It was clear to me when I first came to ACoA that all my skills and efforts weren't enough to solve my personal, financial and health issues. It was also clear when I listened to the Problem and the Solution, and the discussion in the group that ACoA offered me a whole new resource: spiritual support inherent in a fellowship dedicated to healing and to support. With this fellowship's support, I *can* allow myself to admit that my present personal, financial and health issues are rooted in my childhood experiences growing up in a dysfunctional family. For me because the 12 Steps have been a central part of my life for a long time, this admission came quickly, if backwards — from unmanageability to powerlessness (rather than the other way around).

Many newcomers find it harder to connect — to feel the power of the love in the fellowship, or to grasp the unfamiliar process of healing which is demonstrated in the 12 Steps. Or they may find it hard to trust their own feelings of inclusion as "real" or valid, especially since the issues of the past may be so raw and painful to experience again.

We suggest that anyone who is guided (or sent) to ACoA come to at least six meetings before making a decision as to whether or not ACoA is for you. Also make a contact or two, on the phone list. Don't stand alone. Give the fellowship and the process a chance to become familiar and to welcome you. You can always go away again if the program doesn't suit you. Meanwhile keep an open mind, get lots of support, keep coming back and take what you can use!

## STEP TWO

# DISCOVERY

---

*2. Came to believe that a Power greater than ourselves could restore us to sanity.*

---

When I was in high school, the excellent counseling staff tried to help me. During that time, my dysfunctional family centered on me, as "the problem", as I exhibited various acting-out behaviors — absenteeism, a sneering attitude toward some teachers, inconsistent scholastic performance. I was also drinking and using drugs, which I stole from my mother's pharmaceutical selection, and was sexually active — although none of these issues were addressed in counseling. I got through high school — largely through their support. I remember feeling that my counselor cared about me, and I clung to that from week to week — someone I could please about something, even if only schoolwork and attendance, someone who didn't call me hopeless or crazy or dirty.

I didn't have supportive parents. I had the counselors at school, one girlfriend's mother, who was kind and fun to be with, and a teacher or two who encouraged the creative work I did in school.

The dysfunctional man who acted as my father called me names — tramp, whore, bitch — and my mother went along with him, like a competitor for his approval, instead of an ally of mine. She called me names, too — crazy, inconsiderate, selfish — and she supported his efforts to have me thrown into juvenile hall as a wayward teenager, efforts which were foiled by the counselor. I'm not sure how much my mother knew, consciously, about the erotic manipulation he had engaged in with me when I was very small. My mother was a great "deny-er" of what she didn't want to know. But he beat me in her presence and she validated that.

Looking back, I see now that I believed — or wanted to believe — that counseling and counselors could restore me to sanity.

The trouble with the counselors was that they never

raised the real issues — alcohol, drug use, sex and sexual identity. They actually contributed to the denial on these issues by concentrating their efforts on what they saw as *their* realm, issues relating only to school and scholastic issues: attendance, attitude, test scores. Shame and fear kept me from confiding in them, since I assumed they didn't want to know, and that they would reject me if they did find out. I stuffed my disappointment in what I accepted as the limits of counseling, and I gave them what it seemed they wanted and would accept: test scores.

Then after high school, I took the scholarship money in $100 bills and cut out for L.A., with a fifth of brandy in my lap — looking for people like myself, people who wanted to use drugs, wanted to experience some love, who felt a little lost.

I guess, looking back on it, I believed then as I still do now, that fellowship could restore me to stability inside, which is all I know of "sanity" in a modern world. The feeling I had had of the counselor's human concern was a kind of nourishment my dysfunctional family didn't provide, the nourishment of healthy regard and support of one human being to another.

"Parenting", as I understand it now, is a kind of initiation process, where the adult members of the family and the community introduce the children to the ways we human beings support and nourish each other in satisfying our needs and developing our potentials. In effect, "parenting" is the process of introducing others into "fellowship". "Fellowship" means sharing and responding with and to each other. There is such a centered feeling that comes from the experience of that support, support I first recognized in counseling ACoAs back in high school. I was confused by it then, the way ACoAs are often confused by feelings of connectedness and inclusion.

I searched frantically for something or someone to make me centered but in my confusion and denial, nothing ever touched my sense of isolation for long. I had lots of friends — artists, musicians, activists in politics, spiritual seekers.

10

They accepted me. I cared about them, too, although I could never really settle down with anyone or any art for long. The boyfriend I had was a loner, too — and one day he ended up in a mental ward. As much as I recall the highs of lights like diamonds spread against the velvet night, of warm wind in my hair, of poetry and music, I also see myself crying and alone — listening for a car that never stops outside my door or a voice that doesn't call me.

## Finding My Higher Power

I could not have told you then that I was having trouble working the 2nd Step. That was the problem — trying to find a "power greater than myself (to) . . . restore me to sanity" — but I didn't know about the Steps, or the disease of alcoholic families. I knew about insanity though. I searched the self-help and psychology books, looking for my answer, something I could do to make my life complete and satisfying.

I read (according to most psychological authorities), that people who had not had early childhood security, love and socializing, were considered to be more or less human "write-offs", and that there were no easy answers. But I learned a lot of systems, polished my personality and stuffed and denied my childhood: "Things weren't that bad, after all!"

I worked for the Psychology Department at San Francisco State College, took and administered LSD in the mid-60s, accepted an invitation to the core-group at Dr. Leary's estate in Millbrook, New York. Like a lot of ACoAs, while I was looking for an answer to a personal issue, I intensely racked up a lot of colorful experiences and skills. Superficially, I "looked good". Inside I didn't *feel* better — still the same old hole-in-the-gut isolation, for all of my "credits", and so more and more, I fell back into depression and despair. Like my childhood. *Nothing worked for me!*

It was with that basis, *"Nothing works for me"*, that I approached the 2nd Step, once I was introduced to the 12-

11

Step Programs. What "power greater than myself" were they talking about here? And could it work for me, when nothing ever had?

Someone suggested that I try experimentally to see the group as a "power greater than myself". Since these people were seemingly making progress, which I could not do alone, wasn't that "greater than myself"? Experimentally, it was suggested that I bring my own issues out one by one at the meetings to the other members, then all I was asked to do was to look honestly at whether or not, in terms meaningful to myself alone, there were positive changes in my life and experience. Just try the process, they suggested, and see what happens!

That was simple enough. I wasn't asked to "have faith" or any such pious stuff, but only to try the process on myself, then be my own judge as to whether or not it worked for me. As an introduction into the process of spiritual fellowship, that was a method I could understand and try. Of course, I have found that it works for me.

There is no longer a hollow empty loneliness inside my gut today. I'm grateful for that stable, centered feeling. But for the next person, I suggest you do not take my word for it! Instead, as Charlie B., from Lakeport, California, always said, *"You try it for yourself, and see what happens!"*

## STEP THREE

# COURAGE TO CHANGE THE THINGS I CAN

*3. Made a decision to turn our will and our lives over to the care of God as we understood God.*

God, as I understand God, is the life that lives through me. I look within. I see God in the images which speak to me: Guides. Special settings I visit either in imagination or in reality. I find God at the beaches of the California North Coast and on Maui, in the mountains behind Big Sur, or out among the redwoods and the high views across the ridges of the coast Range and Sierras.

I really dislike churches and religion. God isn't "He" so far as I'm concerned, but rather I still have an association of that "He-God" with the dysfunctional man who was my parent: a tyrant of self-will, righteousness, abuse and judgment. This confusion of men with the "He-God" led me to hate and fear men and God for many painful years, and at the same time to feel condemned and dominated by them. It is terribly alienating for me to see God in those old ways of my childhood: Like the dysfunctional parent — tired, useless, greedy, self-indulgent, capable of hate. My mother exhorted me to love both of them, the dysfunctional parent and the "He-God".

Although I know that many people in the fellowship have positive, loving concepts of God who they call "He", I find I still feel rather helpless and uncomfortable, and also angry, when God is characterized as "He". I guess I'm a spiritual feminist!

I like to see God (and visualization is important to me as a means of enhancing the healing) as a woman wearing white or pale turquoise, or as a rangy dark-haired man who is my lover and my mate. I see God as the "little child me" who whispers special secrets in my ear and wants me to always hug her, never go away. These are the sorts of God-concepts that heal me and give me a new strength, to whom I can turn over my life and my will and accept as Guides. I need the reassurance of the Step's "God as we understand God" to be acknowledged in the fellowship because this is personal to me and therefore very sensitive and risky to expose.

I'm afraid of being barely tolerated — rejected, really — because I'm not conventional — not inclined to be a Christian or a member of a church. As an ACoA, it's very difficult for me to stand up for myself and my convictions. I've lied or concealed my vision or masked my understanding; "translated" it, I like to call it. But now I need to bring who I really am to the fellowship and share it. This is very risky, but I need to let you see me because I really need your love; not your love of some partial or false image of who I am, but to know you accept the real me.

In this matter of the God-concept, I have to have the courage and the trust to be honest and know that, scary as it may feel to risk appearing a bit different, it's an important part of healing to trust my Vision and to trust you to accept me, as I come to accept and trust myself.

Once I have made this decision, to be honest instead of manipulative with myself and with the fellowship regarding the God-concept, then I can finally begin to act, not react, with respect to the Third Step.

I began by developing a God-concept in whose care and love I can rely, eliminating old images freely, as the Step suggests I am free to do. Sometimes it is helpful to play a game of "make believe" with myself, to free up my stifled imagination:

"*If there were* a loving God, what would he/she/it be like?"

"*How would it feel* to have a loving God, a personal nurturing Parent or Companion God in my life?"

I work Step Three, rather than just drift along, moving myself toward an atmosphere of increasing spiritual awareness and associated healing.

I can try writing or drawing to develop my God-concept. Reading, looking at pictures, scenery or listening to inspirational talks are also ways I find to "open up". "Opening my heart and mind" is a wonderful habit in itself, since open-mindedness combined with energetic searching leads to growth and to the pleasures of new learning.

As I actively try to move toward a loving God-concept, I find that there are areas of resistance in myself — things about me I find it hard to believe are lovable, or issues in my life I feel I must take care of personally. These old habits of shame/self-blame and control/inflexibility yield better to replacement than they do to attempts to root them out directly.

## Affirmations

Affirmations — that I deserve love, gentleness, support, good times and all the fruits of richness and success in a life of robust good health — are a good way to overcome internal resistances. In areas of specific fear or shame, I can create little *directed* affirmations, that specifically contradict old fears and doubts.

For example, when I was pretty new to 12-Step Programs and was having a lot of difficulty letting a God-concept enter my experience, I had an old, sad self-voice inside that kept saying, "It might work for all you people, but it can't work out for me! I'm just a loser! A hopeless, condemned loser!"

There were other voices, too — angry ones from childhood, screaming at me, "You're no good! You're no damned good at all!" These voices, as it turns out, were what I really believed about myself and my relationship to spirit, deep down inside. To get rid of these "inner bad guys" who were keeping me in a kind of hell and torment, it was suggested that I construct a specific antidote, in the form of affirmations, to each poisonous thought-form, and then let the negative voices and feelings pour out, and as they do so, to shout my affirmations in, replacing and blotting out the harsh old voices.

As I drove home from work, I remember, I would find those inner "hopelessness" tapes starting to run, and I would shout my affirmations with tears streaming, "You win some and you lose some!! God loves me as I am, right now, today!" I must have looked pretty funny to other people in traffic. Maybe they thought I was a real music-lover, singing with my stereo!

It worked, though. It really did — and does, when I find myself falling back into self-negation. Those old harsh voices have "retired", moved out — which is as it should be. I have a right to inner peace of mind. I can't control what other people say, but those inner voices are certainly "fair game" for me to work on for myself!

The trick is to match or exceed the intensity of the negative-messages with well-thought-out antidotes. It's good to keep working on the affirmations to make them as simple and as specific as can be. When I'm up against a challenge now, my inner voices tell me, "You win some and you lose some!", and "God loves me, here and now!", and it helps me take another healing risk, to accept a blessing in my life today.

Finally, in working the Third Step. I ask that my goals and wants be nurtured and made healthy. Much of what I once wanted wasn't good for me, or else it had to be had at someone else's expense. My dysfunctional family didn't help me develop healthy standards for myself, and I find an important part of the Third Step is asking that I be guided in my appetites and desires to want what will truly nourish me.

I don't try to kid myself into thinking I already know, but, rather, I try to become receptive to guidance and suggestion, to trying new courses of action, experimentally, as part of new growth and new beginnings. Doing this is ". . . turning my life and my will over . . ." in a practical way, creating a safer feeling within. I do this often — any time I think about it, pausing to center myself, with a deep breath, opening myself to guidance.

When I've asked for guidance and direction, I move with a growing sense of finding new alternatives to the "old routines", which once so dominated my life. Step Three is the beginning of this practice, the art of opening *to* and accepting a Power which heals, guides and abundantly provides!

# STEP FOUR

# TOWARD REALITY

---

*4. Made a searching and fearless moral inventory of ourselves.*

---

I find the inventory process confusing. My first characteristics to note are that I'm afraid of self-disclosure in
creative matters, also I fear criticism and ridicule.

Since I wasn't sure how to do the inventory, I "hired" a
sponsor, selecting a person with many years of success in
12-Step Programs, a good communicator, and (especially
important to me) someone who was kind, fun-loving and
not judgmental. So here were more characteristics about
myself: I trust in intelligence and a sort of practical success,
a demonstration of the Steps coming to life in one's own
life. That's what I want for me, too, and I am comforted by
someone's modeling (as opposed to being threatened by it,
which is also a common reaction). I also note that I am
attracted to characteristics of gentleness, humor and
tolerance. I take these qualities as indications of security and
strength in a person — which is also what I want for me.

My sponsor supported me specifically in working through
the Steps. My first sponsor, by the way, was Syliva M. ("Big
Sylvia") — a warm, attractive woman who had been 13 years
clean and sober when I met her, and was active in AA, NA,
Al-Anon and OA at that time. She met my criterion very well.
I found it necessary to deal with childhood (ACoA) issues
from the beginning of my recovery, because as it turns out
I am primarily an ACoA, although we did not have such a
focus in 1975-76, when I began my own recovery. Very little
was known about the effects of growing up in dysfunctional
homes and families. Still Sylvia's approach was broad
enough to embrace recovery from any angle, and she, too,
had areas of identification in what was to become Adult
Children of Alcoholics (ACoA).

It isn't a surprise when I think about it that working the
inventory in any 12-Step Program brings out one's ACoA
issues, if there are any.

"Keep It Simple" is a slogan that can be helpful when confusion arises over just what program is really appropriate. I can inventory only one person and one life: mine. All of it (me) is a single fabric of experience and being, from my beginnings in a dysfunctional home through all the compulsions, misperceptions of self and others and maladaptations in result.

I don't gloss over or minimize my own alcoholism or substances-abuse. Neither do I deny my having lived through other people, or my addiction to abusive "power trips" and domestic violence. I use each fellowship and work the Steps as needed. But when I tell my story, there is really only one me and that includes all those behaviors, outgrowths stemming from my coping modes and experiences as a child who wanted to grow up but never really got the parenting she needed in a childhood full of angry, toxic power-mad adults, all of whom have long since died or departed from the home.

I need to see myself becoming unified as a result of 12-Step Programs in my life — not sectioned off into "alcoholic", substance A, B, C or D abuser", "co-dependent", "ACoA", chunks and segments like some jigsaw puzzle (which is how I've often felt about myself, in life!). Fortunately, our program at ACoA, encourages me to become whole, to use the tools available no matter where found, without fear or restriction. I need that sort of tolerance and acceptance and encouragement in a program, and I am grateful to find it in ACoA. Very grateful indeed!

Here is the inventory structure I learned as I apply it: Big Sylvia suggested what is diagrammed in form, in the *Big Book of Alcoholics Anonymous,* pages 64 to 68, and Step Four in the *A.A. 12 x 12*.

First, I write out a balance sheet, *Assets* and *Liabilities.* For me, it is easier to list *Characteristics* first, before deciding whether they are acceptable to me ("assets") or not ("liabilities"). A lot of characteristics seem pretty neutral, at least at first glance, and in many cases I may not be able to get in touch with my feelings about the way I act or think or look at things. So I list them:

*(Using myself as an example:)*

## List of Characteristics About Me

1. Threatened about "putting it out there" for all to see creatively.
2. Afraid of ridicule, criticism.
3. Attracted to intelligence and accomplishment in others.
4. Trust gentleness, humor, tolerance in others.

Now I notice that I've referenced other people in all four of these, either as fear-objects or sources of approval. This gives me a clue about one of my real liabilities: other-centeredness! How can I work on myself if all I think about is other people? So my *number 1* liability is other-centeredness. I write that down on my balance sheet, which I've set up on another piece of paper.

I look closely now at the words "attracted" and "trust". Being attracted to something (or someone) means that I want to experience in myself what I perceive is in that person, thing or experience, so being attracted is being honest about what I want myself, for me.

I know that I have to want recovery and all the good things that I hope for in recovery, so I see that being attracted is an asset, in itself, because it tells me what I want, and therefore, what direction I am moving.

I may decide later that what I'm attracted to isn't so great for me, but unless I am in touch with my wants, I can't even evaluate them. We ACoAs tend to deny all feelings; attraction (desire) is a definite asset I need to encourage myself to recognize and nurture in myself (whether or not I decide to "go after" all that I'm attracted to today).

The other word I look at, trust, feels so good when I can

feel it, that I want to pause a minute and experience how nice it is. Trust certainly is something I want more of, for myself, undefended, open. I take a deep breath and let the word and feeling of trust flow through me. We ACoAs have been hurt, but in recovery, trust is a spiritual golden light that I can choose to experience filling me with peace. I let the word and feeling TRUST become a meditation that I contact when I breathe, and I know this is an asset. I list both attraction and trust as Assets on my balance sheet.

I ask myself what I really mean about myself when I say, "Threatened about 'putting it out there . . .'," and I find that what I "translate" about me is (A) Timid, (B) Suspicious, (C) Rigid, (D) Worthless. It's not so neutral any more. Clearly, these aren't favorite things about myself. I put them under Liabilities.

"Afraid of criticism, ridicule" becomes (A) Sensitive, (B) Weak (intimidated), (C) Suspicious.

What we say we are attracted to in others is always what we identify with. In other words, what I like in someone else is what I feel is truest about me. So applying this formula, "Attracted to intelligence, accomplishment" becomes (A) Intelligent, (B) Able to accomplish (able to *learn*). Those are obvious assets — *if* I'll admit they are really about me!

Also, (A) Gentle, (B) Sense of humor, and (C) Tolerant are assets of mine. All I have to do is have the courage to claim them — which I do by adding them to my asset list.

Looking over what I have written so far, I notice how I lied to myself about me, both regarding Assets and Liabilities. I just couldn't talk, even to myself, about what I'm like without masking it. I either used flowery, confusing language, or else I project what I said, as though it were about somebody else. Seeing this, I added *liar* to my list of liabilities, and I put a star by it, because this was a concealed liability. Things I am deep in denial about (concealing) are major issues for my recovery. Every time I come out of denial about something, I am making a big step toward reality — recovery/discovery. And since I am doing it, I give myself credit in the form of one more asset: Courageous.

I continue to work through my issues, using the balance sheet until I feel completion — knowing I can always come back to this. These processes are all open-ended tools, which are personal assets of mine to keep now, as I include the 12 Steps in my life. I add to my list: (A) Willing to try the tools for growth and change, (B) Hopeful about recovery.

The next part of the inventory process is the Resentment List. I added *how I feel* to the structure as an additional expansion, to encourage myself to *get honest* about my feelings (since the balance sheet has shown me what a great kidder I am about these things). Here's my version, and a couple of examples, taken from myself:

| I resent: | Why? | Affects My: | I feel: |
|---|---|---|---|
| T. | Gossiped about me. Used what I shared with him to try to discredit me. (Present-time event) | Social-relations, Reputation and Self-esteem | *Fear* of abandonment stemming from childhood. *Anxiety* that he will succeed. *Betrayed.* *Angry*, and unsure I can do anything to take care of myself. |
| B. | Sexually molested me. Beat me, ridiculed me, lied about me to family and community to protect himself. (Childhood event) | Sex-relations Family security Social relations Self-concept Self-esteem | *Fear* that my own sexual needs, responses will expose me to pain. *Self-doubt* in my attractiveness and ability to protect myself. *Angry* at being violated. *Hate,* helpless rage and a desire to retaliate. |

25

Constructing this list is a real challenge. I try to be as precise and definite as I can in each column, since confusion and vagueness are old enemies — clouds of ill-smelling smoke that have driven me to abandon myself in the past. I visualize taking myself out to a quiet beach early in the morning, and feel the brisk ocean breeze dispelling the murky haze of confusion about *what really happened to me.* Then I write it down.

It's not important at this point whether or not other family members or other people have come out of denial about any of these issues. It's only important that I do. Often it's very threatening to write down things that happened.

In the case of my molestation, for example, tremendous force over a long period of time was put on me (and others, about me) by the molester to the effect that it didn't happen. Every time I contact the issue, I hear, in my head, "You don't know what you're talking about!" being shouted at me, with a rain of blows and shouting, and being shut up in a room. I feel terribly ashamed, every time I admit the truth! Such twists are common in ACoA's thinking and responses, and so are unfortunately harsh events like these — aspects of what family alcoholism/substances-abuse create in families for children growing up.

Seeing these two resentments written down, it's easy to see that these two resentments aren't equal in weight or power, but that my reaction to the trivial present time event is an over-reaction, stemming from the childhood experience! Lack of perspective and the tendency to go to extremes are liabilities I share with many ACoAs. Looking at "where I came from", I see that I confuse T.'s behavior with B's. B. has been dead for 15 years, by the way, and the trauma many years prior — but the fear remains alive and with me to this day: *F*alse *E*vidence *A*ppearing *R*eal. T. isn't doing what B. did, even if it arouses the same feelings in me. T.'s behavior just isn't such a threat, no matter how sensitive I may be. My problem is the sensitivity — not the gossip.

After finishing the Resentment List, I like to pull any new information on Assets and Liabilities and add those to the

Balance Sheet. In this example, I add Tendency to lose perspective, and Tendency to go to extremes in reactions to my Liabilities List. I add the ability to get objective, to my Assets. Here's my Balance Sheet:

## Personal Balance Sheet

| ASSETS: | LIABILITIES: |
|---|---|
| 1. In touch with my attractions<br>2. Able to experience trust<br>3. Intelligent<br>4. Able to accomplish (learn)<br>5. Gentle<br>6. Sense of humor<br>7. Tolerant<br>8. Courageous<br>9. Willing to try the tools for growth/change<br>10. Hopeful about my recovery<br>11. Ability to get objective | 1. Other-centeredness<br>2. Timid<br>3. Suspicious<br>4. Rigid<br>5. Feel worthless<br>6. Feel weak (intimidated)<br>7. Liar*<br>8. Tendency to lose perspective<br>9. Tendency to go to extremes in reaction<br>(*Formerly a concealed Liability, *from denial!*) |

Surprise! I have more Assets than Liabilities. Can this be true? I have to read over everything to see if there's some mistake.

Having trustworthy support in the Inventory process is very important. In order to go through with this, I have to feel the support that's there for me spiritually. I've learned to use visualizations (one minute vacations) to ground and center myself. I can go anywhere — beach, mountain, car race — which gives me a feeling of peace, be with anyone — loving mother, funny friend, good-looking sweetheart — who comforts me, for just one minute, anytime, anyplace. This is a "quicky" meditation which really works for me. I also rely on human support, a counselor or someone in a sponsorship relationship with me. I find I need a lot of reassurance that I'm not alone.

Like a lot of ACoAs, I find there are padlocks on some doors — blocks against remembering, areas in my mind which are closed and inaccessible. Some whole years of my childhood are "missing" or fragmentary. I don't worry about these. There is no rush. I don't have to use dynamite on myself in ACoA to blast through the blocks and barriers. Instead, I use support. I let it happen, rather than make it happen.

I concentrate on clarifying my goals and vision for myself, what I want out of Recovery. I talk about my goals and vision at meetings and in the fellowship, and I let the process carry me step-by-step, day-by-day. As a part of Inventory I suggest a list or paragraph about what goals are important in recovery — specific and personal, with dollar amounts, dates, names of people involved — any details which make the goals and vision come alive.

Recovery is personal and unique, like we are, but I've always had a lot of difficulty getting clear on what I want for me. My specific goals have grown and modified over the years, and some of what I've thought I'd enjoy has proved not so satisfying, but it's been an important step out of self-negation and denial for me to "get real" about what I want today, and it is a way to build both trust and courage to share my goals for me with you in ACoA.

I find, too, that as I move positively, i.e., toward goals, ideals, the padlocks begin to be removed. Either I find myself motivated down there with a can of oil rattling those rusty old locks and creaky doors, or else events in my life bring me up against stone walls, so that I have to start looking for a way to get over or around in order to get where I want to go. Bricks start to fly. My goals and my vision for myself shape my recovery. This is how I can take charge of my own life, which is my primary goal.

I use the Fears List (page 68 of the *Big Book*) and work through the process as outlined there, including the following Chapter 6, which includes the AA "Promises" — results of beginning the 9th Step.

As a primary ACoA, I have to be careful to stay out of self-negation and self-attack. I bear in mind that the goal in our program is reparenting. I continually come back to seeing myself as the mother/father of a little child who needs my guidance and support, and not the warden of some jail full of hardened crooks. There were times when I could have fit my concept of myself to that tougher image, but that's not ACoA recovery.

I let the little child rely on me. I help her with her goals and establishing standards she can live by in a real world. I don't make her work too hard. Instead, she can take a break whenever she needs to, put her inventory in its folder and go out in the fresh air, the healing sun-clean fresh air. She can admit how hard and painful it is to rattle those old locks, or how scared she gets of what she has to look at behind those bricked-up walls. It's O.K. It's getting better now.

I, the *me* that is an *adult* with a program of 12 Steps, go with that child. She holds my hand. When we find her hidden or locked up in a closet, we let her out. We let her cry. She doesn't have to be alone any more.

My child has all the time she needs to grow. These steps and this family-fellowship are reliable, and as she learns to trust this, through experiencing the love, she finds it fun and challenging to come back to the inventory. It's become a source of comfort, and a touchstone for the magic of growth and change in ACoA recovery.

# STEP FIVE

# INTO THE SUNLIGHT

---

*5. Admitted to God, to ourselves and to another human being the exact nature of our wrongs.*

---

## The Serenity Prayer

*God grant me the serenity*
*To accept the things I cannot change*
*Courage to change the things I can*
*And wisdom to know the difference.*

If I'm going to admit anything to God, I'd better have a God-concept that will accept me, not condemn me. That's my first issue with this Step.

One of the ways my ACoA childhood warps my present day is the "either-weak-or-mean" misconception of authority I formed, including a God-concept that either stood by helplessly or else condemned me, punished me, abandoned me. Anything admitted, it seemed, would be raked up later — used against me, used to mock me. I deeply hated what I used to conceive of as God. In childhood, I tried lying to God. I tried to appear the way I thought I was expected to appear, tried to take on the right look, say the right prayers. I felt like such a phony, trying to look like a little angel while I felt false and angry. I finally ran away and it was years before I stopped running and began my own recovery.

In the Third Step, we are encouraged to ". . . turn our will and our lives over to the care of God as we understand God". I reflect on this again here as I begin Step Five: I need a God that I can really trust.

I find that the Serenity Prayer provides a guideline I can use to reconstruct a healthy concept of spiritual support. I can reasonably ask a loving God for Serenity (Peace of Mind), Courage (Strength: Centered-in-Security, NOT-Fear), and Wisdom (Reliable Good Judgment). I can reasonably expect my loving God to be powerful enough to grant these three things under any and all circumstances, including when I talk to God, admitting all my wrongs. I say the Serenity Prayer over to myself, listening to each word.

Sometimes, I find it helps to go outside and be in nature as I do this, taking in deep breaths of fresh sweet air. I wait until I feel calm, strong and centered, then I begin Step Five.

I see that secrets, false appearances, avoidance and resistance had been my way of life. I coped, survived, held out, escaped — but I had admitted very little in my loneliness and fear. Such hard work! Small wonder I had felt tired all the time!

Now as I take the first two parts of Step Five, I see that I am living my recovery. As I admit these things about me, I am becoming someone who is different because I am doing something different, admitting to myself and God how I survived. I often get stage fright fluttering of butterflies in my stomach at this point, or else I feel anger, almost enough to tear up the whole project. I've come to see either of these reactions as symptoms of returning hope.

## Sharing

When it comes to sharing "... with another human being ... ", it's important that there be no fear of gossip. The sponsorship relationship is the basis I've used for working a formal Fifth Step, an actual going over, point-by-point, incident-by-incident, of what I feel has crippled me. The sponsorship relationship, as I understand it, is a commitment to trust and to grow in trustworthiness. I need this sort of reassurance from another human being as a requirement of doing Step Five.

Just asking someone to work Step Five with me is a tremendous healing risk. I don't rush into it to prove how well I am or to please another person. Yet in my experience the pressure to open up about myself is great. I continue to refer to the centering exercise I have established with the Serenity Prayer, getting calm, strong and clear each step of the way — using spiritual power to guide and direct me in my selection.

Over the years, I've had the experience of sharing some "lesser Fifth Step" at meetings or one-on-one within the fellowship, and having it "get out" and become a subject of gossip. It doesn't seem to matter how long I'm in recovery,

I'm still pretty sensitive and gossip doesn't fail to sting. Since we are committed not to screen our membership, but instead to welcome all who seek recovery, these lapses may occur. I've got comfortable with most of "me", past and present, so there are fewer sensitivities. Now, when I shock or upset someone in the fellowship, I consider living with those sorts of minor upsets as a part of "family life" in my ACoA "family". But part of taking responsibility for my own recovery includes healthy self-protectiveness — not exposing myself to rebuff, insensitivity or rigidity needlessly or carelessly. I'm careful to share my most personal issues with a person I can trust.

The Fifth Step is a step toward a new relationship to others — out of isolation, concealment, fear and into feed-back and response, indispensable ingredients to a balanced point of view. I choose to take this step for me (not as people-pleasing, other-centered behavior). There has been a tremendous sense of relief from this — no more the secret dweller, masked person or person in a world apart.

The biggest surprise came in the response of my sponsor to my sharing. I had shared things I greatly feared might make my recovery impossible, things which I felt would revolt or prompt rejection. I expected severity, a crinkled brow. Instead I found compassion, understanding, gentle-ness. I couldn't believe it. I went so far as to find a different experienced person in the fellowship, to see if I wouldn't get harsher reaction, but once again I was surprised: Gentleness! Compassion! Directed at me!

Finally I began to accept healing human fellowship, and to realize that my old fears were not an accurate estimate of reality. It is as different a world as a sunny morning is different from life lived in a basement without windows, and I can feel the difference in my mind and in my heart.

# STEP SIX

# LETTING GO

---

*6. Became entirely willing to have God remove all these defects of character.*

---

It's said that *people don't change behaviors that work*. That may well be so, but what is successful behavior? This question is the core of Step Six.

Before I began recovery, I had a way of life that survived, coped and escaped. The range of behaviors I employed to accomplish these goals worked pretty well for me, although they didn't lead to joyful contentment. They did, however, get me out of the childhood environment of substances-abuse and tension. I ended my "running and hiding" far from where I began, alone and estranged from other human beings. So long as I had goals of escape, avoidance and denial, my pre-recovery behaviors worked. But I just couldn't live with those old goals anymore. That's precisely what brought me to recovery and to ACoAs fellowship of support. I came to ACoA to change behaviors — behaviors that were making me successfully alienated and isolated.

Starting with the most obvious issues I've already recounted in the previous steps — the very self-defeating behaviors and attitudes which brought me to ACoA in the first place — what are ". . . the effects of alcoholism . . ." over which I find I am powerless? What behaviors and attitudes did I adopt, rooted in frustration and fear in reaction to this powerlessness? Do these old ways that once worked well tend to keep me in a harsher sort of world than I now see is possible for me?

If, for example, I react defensively to any criticism whatsoever because I had a blaming parent, people in my here-and-now world tend to stop giving me feedback. My snappiness or "sadsack" defensiveness is curtailing communication, keeping me behind self-imposed walls of isolation.

Perhaps instead I am attracted to people who pick me apart because they match up with my childhood relationships tending to justify my own real fear of intimacy by criticizing "mankind" in stereotypes or other forms of rigid judgments. I may react with suspicion or clowning to acts of kindness or reaching out I encounter. Aren't I locking myself in a harsher world than it needs to be?

Going over the List of Assets and Liabilities from Step Four, I notice that many of my liabilities were very helpful in the surviving-coping-escaping world of my dysfunctional family childhood. Will these old ways of coping take me where I wish to go in my recovery? Now that I have come this far in the process of recovery and healing experience of fellowship, now that I have begun to experience hope and an expanded vision for my life, which of these old ways that no longer serve me can be let go?

## Positive Self-Image

Focusing on creating a positive self-image for myself, I re-examine my goals for recovery. Why is *my vision* for myself, as a person free of old patterning, free to live in a healthy world today and in my future?

Taking this positive approach is an easy way to begin to see which old behaviors are inappropriate now. It's like looking in a mirror at a healthy human being (my recovery vision for me), and noticing she's carrying what looks like a machine-gun to wipe out dangerous-looking critics. What's wrong with this picture? Maybe she *used* to be a guerrilla commando back in the bad-old-days of childhood, but this machine-gun is pretty clearly not useful now in her otherwise friendly surroundings. A bit too defended?

A couple of years ago I noticed she appeared to be smoking a giant brown cigar. But she's learned now to breathe fresh air again, and as I look at her today, she's ready for a long, relaxing walk with human or animal companions. The cigar is gone — and so are cigarettes.

I notice that my self-image still has roller-skates she can step into at a moment's notice. I'm comfortable with that. She may have an airline ticket in her bag, too, and her luggage appears to be pretty adequate for traveling. But there's no sense of "get-away" about her, now. She just still enjoys the stimulation of change and travel — old carry-over behaviors that don't seem to create problems. I'm the one who takes a look in this, my private mirror, and I'm the one to please, in this phase of my recovery.

I see that what I'm doing now is taking on genuine responsibility for shaping my own character in recovery, coming as I am from within. In healthy families, children are encouraged to develop independence of spirit.

I support myself in these experiments of self-conception and self-imaging as a part of "becoming my own loving parent". I can make a game of it: Put up a real mirror on my wall at home, decorate the frame, use "props" to create visual representations of myself the way I used to be or the way I wish to become. Collage may also be a good medium to try, combining faces, features, hats and other chunks of environments I'd like to try. ("That's me in the great car in the house with a garden view!") A freer imagination, greater sense of self-value, enhanced self-trust are all likely outcomes of this sort of play.

Step Six can be a "giant step" out of Denial, as I actively examine my own behavior and attitude as the cause of my present-day condition regardless how rooted and established this behavior has been, or how well it may have served to "cope with the impossible" of the past. The question remains: Does it serve me now?

Still another approach to Step Six is, "Do I still feel better doing this than I feel not doing it?"

"Do I need this defense, habit or avenue of retreat/escape today?"

If my honest answer is, "Yes!" to such questions and I'm able to share this reservation with a trusted friend, sponsor or counselor/advisor (instead of retreating once again into a secret world of guilt and isolation), then I don't worry or concern myself. Like the image of myself with roller skates handy. Perhaps some people may feel my means of "ready flight" aren't the best indicators of recovery, and, maybe, they have a good point but that's okay. I can live with me today complete with roller skates. *I'm not here to meet other people's standards for recovery, just my own.*

There's real relief in this realization. I'm not going to be pried out of my shell or stripped involuntarily of all defenses in ACoAs application of Step Six. My own desire for the freedom of recovery is the energy which motivates and guides me to voluntarily releasing behaviors and attitudes which no longer serve me and which are no longer necessary to my feeling secure and safe.

This is a very different experience (making choices and decisions with poise) compared to my old way of life in which real perspective always seemed to elude me. Desperation, anxiety and confusion, which were so much a part of any attempt at personal change, begin to be replaced by genuine willingness to experiment with myself and with my life options as a result of my practice of the exercises and techniques of Step Six. I find I am increasingly willing to *let go,* increasingly able to trust the spiritual healing I am experiencing entering my life.

STEP SEVEN

# LETTING GOD

---

*7. Humbly asked God to remove these shortcomings.*

---

A few days ago while I was consideriing what I might say about Step Seven, I happened to be in the "old town" section of the little seaport where I live, an area which is a mixture of quaint Victorian houses and shops and the local Skid Row. I was there to pick up something from a specialty shop, and as I drove away toward home, I noticed a completely hopeless sick looking drunk lying on a streetside bench. It struck me just how forcefully eleven years in 12-Step Programs of recovery have affected my life. "There but for the Grace of God, go I."

I may not have got to that bench (although I'm not sure of that) but I do know — and it's good for me to remind myself — that I felt the despair I saw in that hopeless sad person. I felt disheveled, hopeless, sick, rejected. His disease *is* my disease; the only real difference is recovery.

When I pause to realize how very serious and perilous alcoholism is, how devastating a threat, then it's easy for me to experience genuine gratitude for my recovery: for the fellowship, the Steps, the meetings, the one-on-one. For the influence of renewed hope recovery has meant for me that I'm worth it.

It becomes easier to "count my blessings" from this perspective. I'm a person who's been genuinely given a new chance at life, and I can let go my clutchy tendency to focus on what seems to be out-of-kilter or at cross purposes today in my life and affairs.

Within this "attitude of gratitude" I experience a releasing of held tensions. I let my breathing slow down, my muscles relax. I feel a gentle wave of peace settle around my shoulders as I do this, a warm glow in my chest and stomach. Receptivity opens me as I experience how really cared for and guided I have already been, to have come this far today in my recovery.

As I pause here, reflecting on the blessings of good

fortune which have given me these tools and resources in the Steps and fellowship of ACoA, I can leave off telling God my orders for my life, and I can instead ask that I be guided, clearly and directly, to my highest and most joyful good and greatest usefulness today.

If I am feeling especially remorseful about something I have said or done, or have failed to say or do, I ask to be given a new course or greater insight. But I remember to add something to the effect, "if it be in keeping with my highest good and greatest usefulness and joy today" to the request because, as Shakespeare put it,

> *"We, ignorant of ourselves,*
> *Beg often our own harms,*
> *Which a Wise Power*
> *Denies us for our good; so we find profit*
> *By losing of our prayers."*

> (William Shakespeare, *Antony and Cleopatra*)

Instead of lecturing or begging God, I move instead toward experiencing my feelings fully while consciously directing my mind to reflect upon the reality of my actual recovery. In this way I don't "stuff", justify or rationalize my shortcomings, but instead I let God have them — *and me* — while I strive to remain truly humble in the realization of how lucky and blessed I am to have this program and this fellowship in ACoA. Thus I "give God a chance" while I stay out of God's way by not letting myself fall into old behaviors of controlling or brooding or hurtful self-attack.

# ACCEPTING RESPONSIBILITY

---

*8. Made a list of all persons we had harmed and became willing to make amends to them all.*

---

eviewing the Inventory I made in Step Four, I take a long thoughtful look at my Assets and Liabilities List, my Resentments and my Fears. I notice that there are two casts of characters in my experience, two periods of action and reaction: childhood experiences and present-day experiences as an adult. Those experiences of childhood, ". . . these symptoms of the family disease of alcoholism (which) made us 'co-victims' . . . " largely formed my liabilities, resentments and fears. These have persisted into adulthood, often determining my present behaviors and attitudes.

## Tormentors and Victims

To sharpen the focus I make two lists of names: *Tormentors* (those from childhood: people who hurt me or let me down when I was a dependent child), and *Victims* (people who I've been hard on due to my Adult Child of Alcoholic patterning). In the first list I place the names of all my relatives, including the ones who left home/family while I was growing up for whatever reasons. I include parents, grandparents, brothers, sisters, cousins, aunts and uncles — all my relatives, including categories who were missing.

If I had no brothers or sisters or if the family was spread across the country so that I never saw my relatives, I enter those facts on my list, and how I felt as a result. To this same list I also add school, police, church or other community members/organizations who were woven into the dysfunctional family complex and how they affected me.

I head the list with those who I felt I had *the most right to depend upon,* my mother and father, and then the others in descending order, asking myself, *"Who, as a dependent child, did I have a right to expect to unconditionally love, nurture, guide, support and enjoy the companionship of?"*

How I construct this list is, of course, entirely up to me and reflects the makeup and values of my particular family — and the lacks. If, for example, I was raised by a brother or sister, aunt or grandparent, why was this so (instead of my parents)? If instead I took on a parent's role myself while I was still a child, who let me down and how? Were there aspects of family that got too much emphasis at the expense of others — like an alcoholic parent who demanded a lot of care, absorbed finances which might have been needed by others, or created an emotional draining of family joy, contentment and security? How was I as a dependent child harmed? Which of my resentments, fears and liabilities of character can be traced to each of these Tormentors from childhood?

I look for the exact reasons and circumstances which lead me to ". . . live life from the standpoint of victim . . ." as I have as an ACoA, and I admit how I have blamed these people, the ones who abused substance, the ones who didn't but still weren't able to show me how to live happy and contented lives, the ones who left, the ones who stayed and lied — I blamed them all.

In admitting my needs for unconditional love, nurture, guidance, support and companionship, I cease denying these basic ingredients for health and well-being — an aspect of denial which is common among ACoAs, growing up in families which were too dysfunctional to provide these essentials adequately.

I used to think that if my needs were valid, then my family must be evil, somehow — mean and uncaring — since they didn't/couldn't give me what I needed, tending to act as though my needs didn't exist or were not "real". Sometimes I thought that there was something very "unlovable" about me, or that *I* was evil and didn't deserve to have my needs met. I see now that neither case is true, but rather that my family really was disordered and the people upon whom I had a valid basis for dependence, as a dependent child, just were not able to take care of me.

50

The disease of alcoholism rendered my family dysfunctional. People were either over-burdened with care and responsibility or were driven to escape themselves. Some of them left entirely or died. My needs were valid, *but* in a dysfunctional family such as mine, my needs just could not be met adequately. Not because I was a "bad" or unworthy person, and not because they were bad, but because we were all victims of the disease.

Looking over my list of Tormentors from this perspective, I see how obviously confused, preoccupied, distracted, self-involved, angry, frightened or toxic these people were — perhaps several of these at the same time. No small wonder that I, a child, was left to shift for myself, or that I took on roles far beyond my capacities.

From this perspective I see now what the purpose of constructing this list has been in terms of my recovery: *I am stepping right out of the role of Victim!* I listed my Tormentors to see how people have harmed me, only to find that those "old meanies" were, themselves, suffering from the same disorder which brought me to ACoA and to these Steps.

Now in ACoA the solution suggests that I can ". . . become my own loving parent . . ." as I am in a sense becoming this very moment, in guiding myself through this process of recovery in the Steps, and in opening myself to the support and nourishment of the fellowship of ACoA. With these resources that I accept into my life, I can release these Tormentors, and I can even feel compassion for them, without negating the needs I had or glossing over or denying the weaknesses, mistakes or excesses of their past behaviors — back when I was their responsibility and they let me down. These poor suffering fellow beings had lost (or never found) the guidance of a Loving Parent, such as we experience in the fellowship of ACoA. My dysfunctional family was cut off from this love.

I can free my parents, siblings and others in authority from the burden of blame I had heaped upon them *because* my needs can be met. I am not hopeless as I once feared. In

51

fact, my needs are being met as I take up this responsibility for connecting with "... a Power greater than ourselves (which) could restore us to sanity".

As I release the anger and fear, grief for family members lost comes over me. I wish there had been recovery long years ago when I was a child. So much love and enjoyment were missed. People aren't replaceable like cars or overcoats. I miss my family members who have died or gone. I'm sorry for us all, as a family and as children of a loving God. We lost our way, back there, for a while. But I no longer have to live out my life in fear or longing for "what might have been". As I find the willingness to go forward, I have a "Loving Parent" in ACoA and a fellowship of brothers and sisters to support me as I guide myself into a world of new possibilities — free of Tormentors finally.

Now I reflect, "How have I harmed *these* people — the ones who let me down due to dysfunction?"

Blaming them — for my own weakness, anger, fear and out-of-balance attempts to compensate — is one harm done, although I see that I could hardly have kept from doing it until I found a way to get my unmet needs fulfilled through my own recovery. But can I stop blaming them now, since I've found a way out of the maze and mess of dysfunction? Am I willing to make these amends?

I go over the Tormentors list again, noting how each affected me, as a contributor to my disease. I ask myself, "Am I entirely ready to take over this aspect of my own parenting with the help of ACoA?" If my answer is, "Yes", then I ask myself, "Am I entirely ready to make amends to this person — to stop blaming him/her once and for all? Am I free of the need to see this person as Tormentor and myself as Victim?" If my answer is, "Yes", I go on throughout the entire list.

If I find I cannot honestly stop blaming and feeling injured by someone on my list, I make a note of it and place that person or group on a list requiring further work. Our program, I remind myself, is one of improvement, not perfection, a day at a time! If I can't release a hurt or grief today, that's okay. I review Step Seven's commitment to let God have control of my recovery, rather than try to make it happen in some preconceived way that I have devised. It's important that I have patience with myself.

When I am ready to genuinely release the past and to step free of the old role of Victim myself, then I take a look at the list of personalities in my present adult life. I call these people "My Victims", because I admit I have been dysfunctional myself as a result of my disorder.

I list spouse or lovers, children, relatives (including any from the former "Tormentors List", in this new context as Victims now of my adult dysfunction). I also include co-workers, and all people in my life — including those I've pushed away, cut off, rejected or run away from. Who, I ask myself, has a right to some level of unconditional love, nourishment, guidance, support or companionship from me?

I am entirely free to set up this list any way I choose. This is one of the great freedoms of recovery in ACoA, the right I have to live toward my own ideals and goals that I establish for myself. I go over the work I have done in the previous steps in establishing goals for my own life in recovery, paying special attention to what I have said I wish for in relationship to other people. Who I feel has a right to my love, care and support will largely determine who, if anyone, will be close to me, and how close.

If my present life has few people in it, or if there are "blank spots" in certain types of relationships, I ask myself why this is so, and whether there's something which has persisted from my dysfunctional childhood which has made me freeze or block out certain kinds of connections which most human beings enjoy? Is there intimacy in my life? Family connections? Friends? Pleasant ties in the community through work, service, creativity? Or are there certain areas which are greatly over-valued, such as too much work or service, or too great an obsession with romance or family responsibilities?

Step Eight is probably the greatest single step an ACoA can make in recovery, since our very disorder is centered in our flawed self-concept and unbalanced relationships which stemmed from childhood. All the Steps which lead to this undertaking create a framework within which we can entirely restructure our attitude toward ourselves and all those whose lives we touch. From this new standpoint as a free person, no longer a victim, I am literally transforming myself and transmuting my own history from a chronicle of pain and tragedy to a fund of understanding, compassion and strength: Straw (and much worse than straw) to gold.

In such a potentially thorough-going undertaking, I do my best to be methodical. I take my time. I bypass the impulse to say, "I've only hurt myself " (although it certainly is true), since this step asks me to examine my relationship with people. After all, I knew how desperately lonely I was, when I came to ACoA. This is the Step where I try to find out why. From the standpoint of a person free to enter a world of satisfying relationships, the way I can do this is to see how I've been keeping myself lonely.

Have I denied various needs, first to myself and then to others? Did I feel that love was always conditional or did I entirely refuse to make or accept commitments? Did I make them, but then run out or make myself unavailable? Was I disloyal out of fear when a friend or family member had a right to expect my support in an argument? How did my liabilities shape the way my relationships took form or failed to endure?

I give my best efforts to examining my role in each and every one of my adult relationships, looking for the keys which will unlock new possibilities. This is a role I have to take in my own life if I wish to have the fruits of recovery in my relationships stemming from a re-evaluation of myself.

There may be a great deal of confusion in attempting to see how I have harmed, denied and victimized people in my life. After all, I lived my life as a victim myself! How could *I* be guilty of such behavior, especially since the people around me were often the worse behavers? I have to take a real good look at why I chose these people. Was it to make myself look good? Did I key on certain weaknesses which made me appear strong? Did I harm these people by showing them up?

Rather than launch off into a bout of self-attack, I bring myself up with this reminder from The Solution: "This is a spiritual program based on action coming from love . . . " It is important that I extend this love to me, so recently a victim, and extend to myself the blessings of compassion and understanding I have come to be able to extend to those who were formerly "Tormentors" in my life.

My goal in Step Eight remains to search out just how I've harmed people — neglected them, rejected them, projected old fears and angers upon them — with a view to becoming entirely willing to make amends to them all, *not* to punish myself or to writhe in self-loathing or guilt about these past mistakes. It's enough to become willing today to break the old patterns in my life, and to make it right with each of those I've wronged here in my heart. In this way, then, I begin to experience the healing of forgiveness through the practice of Step Eight.

I go through my list of Victims now, just as I did with Tormentors, but this time I look at *my* behavior in terms of what I decide was or is my responsibility to each person on my list. I ask myself the same questions, as to my willingness to accept responsibility in each of these relationships. For the first time in my life I am acting as a free person, no longer a victim in relationship to other people.

# ACTION COMING FROM LOVE

---

*9. Made direct amends to such people wherever possible, except when to do so would injure them or others.*

---

For my kind of ACoA the wording of Step Nine brings up feelings of guilt and responsibility: "What have I done? How have I hurt you? Am I in trouble?" Clearly making amends and possibly injuring people rings some old bells in my heart and mind, sets old rabbits running in reaction. Before I panic and begin caretaking, appeasing or defiant reactions, it's time for me to quiet my heart and my thinking and seek calmness, poise and a balanced perspective.

I can unify my perspective by reviewing my progress so far, from Step One through Step Eight, allowing the calmness and centering tendency of the Steps to melt away the reflexive panic and guilt which Step Nine tends to trigger.

Step Nine is not an isolated activity, not like being made to go in and apologize to a raging substance abuser, or an attempt to manipulate someone for one reason or another. No, Step Nine, when seen as part of the process of recovery/discovery, is a wholesome result of restructuring my self-concept. I don't do Step Nine out of fear, dread, guilt, shame or competition. I do Step Nine for me out of action coming from love.

As I review my progress through the Steps, I see how each Step organically moves my awareness along, like the process of a growing plant. Like a seed entering the fertile ground, I applied the first three Steps, immersing myself completely in the healing and spiritual support of ACoA, so that my hard outercoating could be softened and my inner life could expand and sprout, pushing upward toward the radiance of Light.

Then in Step Four I began to explore and discover my individuality, forming the embryo, leaves and stem, of this plant, me, which entered the realm of visibility as I unfolded myself in the sunlight of Step Five, extending and refining my self-expression in Step Six. I expanded my leaves and grew tall with the increasing receptivity of Step Seven, letting the Life Force shape and nurture me.

Finally in Step Eight I set buds which in Step Nine become flowers of expression, fruits of my own growth. The entire process is one of self-development, self-unfoldment. There is nothing in it of appeasement or reaction.

Although a flower may be extremely beautiful and sweet or a fruit delicious, I always remind myself it is springing from the richness of its life — fulfilling its own destiny — and not serving needs of mine when I am breathless and touched in a fragrant garden. It's serendipity with which I am blessed — delighted and well-fed. And as I flower and fruit, as I move through the process of the Steps, I bloom and nourish others who share this patch of garden with me where our roots entwine, through kinship or association, but I do it for myself. This is action, as I understand it, springing from love.

After I have calmed and centered myself with this little meditation, I begin exploring the particular fruits and flowers of my own recovery, seeing how I can extend my self-expression in the spirit of Step Nine, to making direct amends wherever possible, except when to do so would injure others.

## Promises

In the AA program Step Nine is associated with "The Promises", from pages 83-84, *The Big Book of Alcoholics Anonymous,* with The Promises representing the fruits of recovery, in a similar organic process of recovery from alcoholism.

Many ACoA groups have adopted these as part of the informal literature of ACoA. Reading over "The Solution" from ACoAs own literature, I notice that much of what is included implies similar Promises for ACOAs

In the spirit of "Keep It Simple", I set these down — not to negate or invalidate in any way AAs Promises, but rather to focus my understanding of recovery's potential in ACoA, my primary program of recovery.

I count 22 Promises, from "The Solution":

1. ACoA becomes a safe place for us.
2. We find freedom to express ourselves.
3. We free ourselves from the shame and the blame carryovers from the past.
4. We become adults who are no longer imprisoned by childhood reactions.
5. We recover the child within, learning to accept and love ourselves.
6. We risk moving out of isolation.
7. Feelings and buried memories return.
8. We gradually release the burden of unexpressed grief, slowly moving out of the past.
9. We learn to reparent ourselves with gentleness, humor, love and respect.
10. We see our biological parents as instruments of our existence, and accept our actual Parent as a Higher Power who some of us choose to call God.
11. Action and work — using the Steps, the meetings, the telephone — heals us.
12. We share our experience, strength and hope with each other.
13. We learn to restructure our sick thinking.
14. We release our parents from responsibility for our actions today.
15. We become free to make healthful decisions as actors, not reactors.
16. We progress from hurting to healing to helping.
17. We awaken to a sense of wholeness we never knew was possible.
18. We come to see parental alcoholism as a disease.
19. We learn to keep the focus on ourselves.
20. We love and encourage each other, no matter what.
21. We ask that you accept us as we accept you.
22. As the love grows in us, we see beautiful changes in all our relationships.

Some of these Promises relate to our past, to childhood and parenting issues which remain a fundamental foundation for our growth, restructured now in durability, where they once seemed based in sand or mud which might hold us fast or suck us under. Other Promises speak of healthy freedoms, altered attitudes and outlooks that provide sources of strength for our growing selves now present in here-and-now One-Day-At-A-Time reality. Only five of these ACoA Promises directly tie to our relationships to other people. These are (12.) "We share our experience, strength and hope with each other;" (16.) "We progress from hurting to healing to helping;" (20.) "We love and encourage each other, no matter what;" (21.) "We ask that you accept us as we accept you," and (22.) "As the love grows in us, we see beautiful changes in all our relationships".

Amends to other people from this ACoA perspective largely centers around issues of (a) Sharing myself (experience, strength, hope) (b) Unconditional love ("no matter what") (c) Acceptance (d) Honest acknowledgement of good (as opposed to denial, creating false appearances or hypocrisy). Nothing of the people-pleasing, coercion or caretaking behaviors which so many of us had associated with amends or apologies is implied. Instead we are asked to become honest in our repsonses, loyal and caring, and to *witness* the changes. Bearing this perspective in mind, then, I consult my Step Eight list.

At the top of my list is a class of people who I once called my Tormentors, those who were responsible for my parenting when I was a dependent child and who let me down, neglecting or abusing me.

I made one big step in my amends to these people when I came to see them as fellow sufferers, co-victims of this disease from which I am presently recovering. When I saw my way out of living life from the standpoint of Victim, I released these people from blame — by realizing that they simply were unfunctional, as I was, too, before I found a way to recover in ACoA.

Now, in Step Nine, I see that *"Honor thy father and mother"* can be seen as a combination of not letting their weaknesses and dysfunction due to the disease interfere with my living a full and happy life today and on the other hand, of becoming secure enough in my own present recovery to actually go back and claim and acknowledge the gifts and strengths which they did give me, even through the pain. It wasn't all bad, after all!

What kinder amends can a child make to a parent who neglected or abused than to recover — becoming free of suspicion, malice, self-pity and fear — and to let my recovery become a source of potential joy; joy in the acknowledgment that health and the power of Love is greater than old mistakes, however grave and violent they may have been? If I'm okay, then their failures weren't as bad as they feared. Although I recover for myself, my recovery is a kind of gift I give my family as well.

Looked at this way, ACoAs list of Promises becomes a little more comprehensible. Our greatest amends are centered in our work to free and strengthen the lost, battered child within ourselves. From the healing of this child-self emerges potential for nourishment which lay buried, useless, latent, withheld from even ourselves. No one but me can put into life my contribution, however humble, however great.

## Self-Love

I keep the focus on myself, not out of selfishness, but out of self-love, in taking responsibility for my own parenting, I do this because I've come to understand that concentrating on my own healing is the kindest and most generous starting place for me.

Just as ceasing to live my life from the standpoint of victim was a revolutionary change in Step Eight, I see that centering myself in action coming from love — beginning with self-love — is a similarly revolutionary change in the basis of my behavior here in Step Nine.

Now, continuing down my list, I see where my disease has led me to withhold my sharing, unconditional love from each person on the list, to create a false front of deception which confused these issues. What forms of behaviors did I use? Disappearing acts? Creating uproars or diversions? Generating crisis — financial, social and/or sexual? Do I seek "high moral ground", establish a "look good" or play the mental or financial "hot shot" in order to distance myself? Or have I been a "sadsack" energy drain, fear-monger, gossip, envier or otherwise got bigger by tearing someone down? I get as specific and as concrete as I can in terms of these behaviors and attitudes, remembering that, as is the case with all of my recovery, I am doing this *for myself.*

It's important not to work alone in this phase of Step Nine. We ACoAs are more likely to go to extremes in our thinking and acting with other people than most people, and it is generally true that people tend to "work out" their amends, develop alternatives to non-fruitful courses of action by sharing and interacting among a peer group. *Not* doing this is one of the characteristics many ACoAs have in common, an aspect of the Problem we share in common. It's an important aspect of our recovery to get into the habit of confiding with someone about our plans, seeking feedback and learning to develop a balanced point of view. Nowhere is this more important than in Step Nine.

The concern in Step Nine to make amends ". . . except when to do so would injure them or others" is specifically intended to caution us against hasty and ill-considered action when it might strongly affect other lives.

Take, for example, a case where I may have pushed a lover (or mate) out of my life due to my ACoA based suspicions or fears. I may see that today and feel terrible remorse about the rejection I inflicted on that person. Perhaps I still have romantic feelings for them, too. Should I just get in touch, get out the truth? What about third parties who may presently be involved with one or the other of us? What about my own real goals here — am I just trying to unload a lot of guilt or do I really want to give this person something, and if so, exactly what is that?

It's easy to see how working on these sorts of issues alone is likely to lead to confusion and perhaps serious mistakes. It's important in Step Nine to talk over your proposed amends with someone — a sponsor or a counselor — someone who will give you honest feedback, no matter what.

If I experience panic or confusion when it does come time to go out and offer my amends, or if anger seems to reassert itself and threatens to take control of the situation, I take myself through the meditation of the growing plant that I outlined at the beginning. Or if I'm in the midst of the interchange, I do the quick Step Five centering technique — take in one or two deep breaths and ask God for present Calm, Courage and Clarity, while visualizing any source of beauty or joy I choose.

I remind myself, again, "I do this amends for me and what you choose to do with what I offer is entirely up to you — not my business although I wish you well."

Unless I am sure that the person I am offering amends to is open to meditations such as these, I usually do not do any of this out loud, since I might be misunderstood.

In talking to the person I am offering amends to, I stick to specifics as much as I can. I let them know how I misunderstood them or the situation, or over-reacted or whatever it may have been. Then I explain my new insight, based on my recovery in ACoA, trying to let them see how my standpoint is no longer that of victim in life and what my new perspective leads me to offer — action coming from love. If there is some difficulty getting the communication clear, I offer to give it some time, rather than demanding instant response.

With a little practice I've come to find it possible to experience miracles of healing in relationships that I feared were lost, through the application of this Step. So will anyone who is willing to try this simple process — action coming from love.

## STEP TEN

# ONE DAY AT A TIME

---

*10. Continued to take personal inventory, and when we were wrong, promptly admitted it.*

---

Step Ten starts with the proposition of *continuing* the process established in the previous nine steps, a process which I've experienced as so dynamic that it's left me feeling like a person walking in fresh sand, making new footprints along an unexplored shore.

I'm a newcomer in a world which has itself seemed to change as a result of incorporating these Steps and this ACoA program into my way of life. Or perhaps it's the other way around — perhaps it's more that I've immersed myself, surrendered, begun to be a joined organic part of this program and this fellowship?

In either case, the old careworn depressed scene I came from has fallen away, been left behind, as though I left a medieval city, sailing my way on a steady wind past reefs and dangers to a warmer, safer world, a world where the sand is fresh and everything seems somehow younger and renewed.

At the beginning these Steps, like northern waters, may have seemed somewhat forbidding, perhaps cold or murky deep. It was hard to trust myself to a frail-seeming fellowship and begin. But I had such a need to find a way free, to leave that dark lost structure of the past, I had to chance it and wade in.

Now sometimes I feel like I'm in a glass-bottomed boat when it comes to these same Steps. I watch with a peaceful concentration as visions emerge, and I contemplate deeper possibilities, richer opportunities than I had previously imagined, like a tropical seascape with fantastic fishes and coral castles amid a flow of seaweed and slow-moving jellyfish. Where, I wonder, did the water change, from cold to warm? From murky dark to turquoise?

This process of the first nine Steps which I have established for myself — or that has somehow become established within me — has brought me through to this safer-seeming world. However hesitantly or quickly I have made this first crossing, I see that something *more* than the energy I've put in has come back to me. I've come further than I've brought myself.

Now, Step Ten asks me to continue, to go on up this beach, enter this fresh world, continue making progress.

But can't I just stop here? It's so much better than it was, can't I just relax now, soak up some sun, congratulating myself for my good efforts, count my many blessings and wear my recovery like a garland of flowers? The idea of continuing sounds like work. Is there never to be a time when I've arrived?

Recovery/discovery is a process, not a place or achievement to be recorded on a plaque. Recovery is a living thing alive in me, one day at a time, if it is alive in my life. If I settle back to bask on this sunny beach I've imagined for myself, it may be I'll find I've bought myself a roundtrip ticket. I may wake up to find myself rounding those old reefs, on my way back to what I thought I'd left behind forever. It's not a matter of frantic struggle or hard work continuing in recovery. Instead, it's a matter of cultivating an on-going way of life, accepting newness and change instead of shutting down or closing myself off from growing.

That tendency to settle or to say, "Isn't this enough?", are ways my old habits seek to reassert themselves. My disease will step back in, retake control and it will take me back to those old familiar landscapes (however much I may have hated them) if I get too complacent, or if I allow my tendency to become "an expert" to fool me into self-forgetfulness.

Step Ten is more like a reminder to keep up an exercise program which has given me a skill which I enjoy, one which I would lose if I failed to continue practice. Just as I have taken on responsibility for seeing to my own healing, exposing myself to the forces of healing in this program of recovery, I'm the person who must decide to continue with this process.

Step Ten is the keystone of the One-Day-At-A-Time program, a habit we have already begun to integrate in moving through recovery this far, having got through the first nine steps at least once. Step Ten is a continuation of the process, a method more than anything else which allows me to keep this healing process alive and growing, not fading or losing force, as so many growth-process undertakings tend to do because they lack the component of continuing.

If I can now welcome Step Ten as an opportunity, rather than some dreary obligation, then, my next level of resistance is around the issue of time. Am I supposed to spend all my efforts inventory-ing myself, constantly looking over my shoulder? This resistance I realize is another mask of my old way of life reasserting itself: never giving time or attention to my own needs, certainly not on a regular basis.

Certainly, in taking charge of my life and responsibility for my continuing recovery, I can make a little time for self-contemplation. A few minutes at some specific time each day, before a meeting or before bed or during a mid-afternoon break is one approach. Another is the Spot Check approach, to be used in situations of stress, a sort of momentary retreat to re-establish my priorities. Perhaps occasional weekend retreats to go over my ACoA issues and to re-evaluate my goals is an option I'll select, to combine with one or both of these quicker methods. To establish a program which includes Step Ten we need a combination of regularly committed time with an outline or checklist to help maintain the focus.

## Self-Survey

The usefulness of some sort of outline for a brief self-survey depends, of course, on the checklist's being specific to my ACoA issues. For Step Ten, I don't want a checklist which simply lists a bunch of goals or projects, although I may want to keep track of those sorts of things as part of my vision for my own growth. But for my personal inventory, I find it helpful to refer to the key ACoA issues, as I understand them from "The Problem" and, based on this, I've made a Spot-Check Reference and a Step Ten Key-Issues Outline. The Spot-Check Reference is a list of six questions, put in positive terms, taken from six important ACoA "Problem" issues. These same six issues are diagrammed more thoroughly in the Step Ten Key-Issues Outline.

I use the Spot-Check Reference often. I cultivate the habit of pausing in the midst of my daily efforts and activities to ask myself these questions, especially when I begin to feel rushed or under stress. If I find that I am having trouble in one of these areas, I make up an affirmation to help me through the current situation, and then later when I have set aside time, I go over the area, utilizing the Outline. Using the Outline and sharing with others in the program (or in counseling) along with participation at meetings guides me over a period of time to seeing emerging aspects of my childhood patterning. This reveals itself through current events, which I can recommit to the healing process, often beginning with Step One. I find I am able to both live and grow in the present and also make continuing progress on my deeper, dysfunctional childhood-based issues, without being overwhelmed. By combining affirmations with self-reflection, and by setting aside times when I allow myself more freedom to open up to deeper layers of my issues as they continue to emerge, I continue to grow.

Here are the checklist and outline in their current form:

## Spot-Check ACoA Reference

Right now:

1. *Am I able to communicate* my feelings/ideas/needs?
2. *Am I comfortable* with my drives/appetites?
3. *Am I in touch with my* independent *identity?*
4. *Am I acting from love* in my relationships?

5. *Am I feeling my feelings, conscious of my thoughts?*
6. *Am I in touch with a peaceful center* inside myself?

## Step Ten Key-Issues Outline:

Over the past *(time period — day, month, etc.)* have I experienced:

I. **Isolation:**
  A. Am I able to *communicate* my feelings/ideas/needs?
  B. Do these behaviors/feelings block my communication:
    1. Uneasiness (lack of trust, fear of being judged)?
    2. Defensiveness (fear of loss, rejection)?
    3. Appeasement (fear of anger, abandonment)?
    4. Defiance (fear of being controlled, confined)?

II. **Obsession:**
  A. Am I *comfortable* with my drives/appetites?
  B. Are these obsessive behaviors or compulsive needs present:
    1. Alcoholism, drug abuse, food abuse, gambling, sex abuse?
    2. Other people's compulsions taking over my energy/attention?
    3. Drive for money, power or prestige taking over?

III. **Victimization:**
  A. Am I in touch with my independent *identity?*
  B. Do I perceive myself/others as:
    1. *More* powerful?
    2. *More* needy?
    3. Rescuer?
    4. Tormentor?

IV. **Disloyalty:**
  A. Am I acting from *love* in my relationships?
  B. Are my actions toward others centered in fear, manifesting as:

73

1. Avoidance?
2. Rejection?
3. Manipulation?
4. Demands?

**V. Dishonesty:**
    A. Am I feeling my feelings, *conscious* of my thoughts?
    B. Am I denying my feelings/thoughts/attitudes by:
        1. Shutting them down (stuffing)?
        2. Shutting out information (meetings, reading)?
        3. Not sharing?
        4. Lying?

**VI. Distraction:**
    A. Am I in touch with a *peaceful center* inside myself?
    B. Am I distracted or preoccupied by:
        1. Anger?
        2. Anxiety?
        3. Confusion?
        4. Pressure?

Step Ten also asks that I develop the habit of admitting error in myself as quickly as I'm able to see it. Utilizing these inventory tools on a regular basis is really helpful, I find, in getting free of old ideas, old behaviors and attitudes which may have persisted a long time unnoticed. Coming up with new behaviors is a creative process, however. If I can admit I've made a mistake, then I'm in a position to get feedback and ideas on alternatives.

I had so few alternatives before I began recovery. It remains a matter of discovery and creative effort for me to come up with new ways to deal with situations I always avoided in the past. I often find myself asking people's opinions as to just what behavior is appropriate — neither aggressive nor appeasing, but assertive, clear-headed and whole-hearted. It certainly isn't automatic, making behavior choices. I often feel at risk, but I've come to seek out and to accept the support I now realize exists for me, and with this support I'm beginning to accept discovery and change as healthy parts of my life.

STEP ELEVEN

# FIRST THINGS FIRST

*11. Sought through prayer and meditation to improve our conscious contact with God, as we understood God, praying only for knowledge of God's will for us and the power to carry that out.*

ACoA is a spiritual program (see the last paragraph of the Solution) — not a therapy or mental health practice. Although we are encouraged to make use of therapy, psychology, medical advice and any other tools which may be of help in our recovery/discovery, the *core* of ACoA (and of all Twelve-Step Programs) remains spiritual. "Our actual parent," the Solution affirms, "is a Higher Power whom some of us choose to call God. Although we had alcoholic parents, our Higher Power gave us the 12 Steps of Recovery."

In Step Eleven we are asked to adopt a systematic practice (through prayer and meditation) aimed at very specific spiritual goals:

(1) improved conscious contact
(2) knowledge of God's will
(3) power to carry that out

Before cringing at the prospect of this immense new undertaking, it may be a good idea to reflect on the fact that the goals of Step Eleven are very similar in tone and direction to the Serenity Prayer, which most of us join in on at each meeting without resistance. If I take the view that experiencing peaceful calm and centered serenity is a form of conscious contact with God, that "courage to change the things I can" is very like "power to carry that (God's will) out," and that "wisdom to know the difference" is similar to "knowledge of God's will for us", then Step Eleven seems more of a case of admitting what we've been doing in ACoA and committing to keeping it up as a practice.

Pausing at this point to review the spiritual aspects of our program — how our healing and re-parenting of our self-concepts is centered in developing acceptance of a Loving Parent, and not just the result of our hard work — may be a good move.

Step One asks us to admit that we are personally powerless to solve or escape problem issues which make our lives out of control, unmanageable. Step Two asks us to open up the possibility, the hope, that there is a Power in the universe which can heal us, restore us to sanity. Step Three offers us the opportunity to dump our "old ideas" associated with the word "God", and to begin to build a healthy, nourishing concept of a Parent, an ally we can trust with our will and our lives.

Without establishing a spiritual foundation by working through and opening to the principles of these first three steps, the fearless and thorough moral inventory which we attempt in Step Four is felt not to be really possible, from the point of view of the Twelve-Step Programs. The feeling that we need a spiritual grounding in order to be either fearless or thorough is a fundamental basis of ACoAs approach, differing with many therapy approaches. These may emphasize insight, personal power or reliance on human (therapist) support. ACoAs approach includes insight, commitment and human elements, but its healing power is grounded firmly in the spiritual resources we seek to develop and expand, both in personal application of the principles expressed in the Steps, and also in the acknowledgment of the concept of fellowship, as distinct from group-therapy or from associations which have a practical basis, such as work or hobby interests held in common.

Fellowship is spiritual support which is based in universal brother/sisterhood, fellow-feeling — in the sense that we *do* share a common Spiritual Parent or are joined somehow in the Great Spirit of Life. (We are free, of course, to give this unifying sense any name or description we like.)

In Step Five, we begin to live our revised spiritual conception: We open up to the God of our understanding, and we also open up to fellowship as a force for healing. We trust another person to share enough common ground with us to hear our confession, our secrets — secrets we may have felt cut us off, set us outside the human family (if there was such a thing).

Therapy often includes components of discussion, sharing, exploration of fears, searching for insight similar to Step Five's practice. But the element of release, the emotional lift, may not be there in therapy or it may not be an experience that we can build on or sustain.

Step Six encourages us to build toward an ideal, to open up in an enlarging way to the possibility of development and change in ourselves and in our lives. And Step Seven reminds us to allow the Spiritual Element the freedom to guide us, as opposed to establishing fixed, inflexible goals for ourselves since these must always be *less* than is ultimately possible in a living recovery.

In Steps Eight and Nine we take the position that our real parent is a Higher Power now. So we release those who let us down, hurt us or were inadequate in our actual childhood, releasing ourselves at the same time from living life from the standpoint of victims, since we acknowledge that we have a power source, ACoAs Loving Parent — a source of healing, freedom and a growing vitality which gives us a way of life our human families lacked, at least as it applied to us and our growing up.

We encourage this Power to guide us into new behaviors, new attitudes, provide us insights in healing the hurts we caused. We ask for clear understanding, courage and heart-centered regard (instead of reaction) in all our relationships, past and present. Again and again, we come back to the principles we are considering in Step Eleven: conscious contact (action coming from love), combined with knowledge of God's will (as regards our behavior toward other people), and power to carry that out (making amends, establishing new behaviors).

As is the case with therapy, we take responsibility for our lives in the present, reaffirming this commitment by applying Step Ten's continuing "one-day-at-a-time" approach to our lives and to new issues as they emerge. Unlike therapy, however, we take on this responsibility by an expansion of our self-concept to include a dimension of personal spirituality as a source of power. It is this Spiritual

Resource which gives our commitment force which we admitted we *lacked* in Step One.

## Let Go, Let God

My misunderstanding of "authority", warped in childhood by the inconsistency of human models in a dysfunctional home, may have led me to fear that I might lose my personal identity by relying on a "power greater than myself". Relying on those human authorities have been disastrous, foolish, heartbreaking, after all.

In ACoA, as I move through the steps, I gain a new perspective on "authority". *Spiritual Authority,* a Power greater than human authority, replaces those unreliable, non-nourishing, defensive or attacking forms of "authority" which I was wise to mistrust. A little at a time I shift into relaxed acceptance of this new concept of authority, strengthening and freeing my personal identity as I reduce my burden of fear, mistrust, self-doubt and confusion.

As I make this transition, from reliance on or reaction to human power and authority, to drawing on and being guided by Spiritual Power and Authority, my recovery becomes established on a basis which is entirely revolutionary, a basis which is only limited by the boundaries of my understanding and willingness to grow.

Looked at in this way, seeking improved conscious contact, knowledge of God's will and power to carry that out becomes a clear and definite priority, a "First Things First" endeavor.

Once I've admitted that spiritual growth, guidance and centeredness are my primary goals in recovery, then the rest of my priorities and commitments can fall in line. My marriage, career/creative interests, other family members and friends remain important to me, but none of these will do well unless I keep my priorities straight. I need my Spiritual Resource to guide and empower me in all my relationships and efforts in life. It's a case of "Seek ye first the kingdom . . ." keeping "First Things First".

But "prayer" when I was a child growing up in my dysfunctional family, was a word associated with painful, hopeless pleading with an unresponsive diety. I used to "pray" to be rescued or to have some family member changed, removed. I begged, offered "deals" ("I'll do such-and-such, God, if you'll get me out of this"), or else I might tear myself down, thinking God wanted me to admit how really wrong and sinful I was, as though that would make God willing to help and rescue me or change a family member. "Prayer", as I understood it then didn't work for me, just as "God", as I understood God, was confused with my dysfunctional parents — inconsistent, demanding, judgmental, inaccessible or violent.

Just as Step Three offered me the opportunity to begin establishing a healthy understanding of God, I am free in Step Eleven to take a look at my "old ideas" stemming from associations in my dysfunctional family upbringing with the concept of "prayer".

I really needed to do this re-evaluation because those "old ideas" had turned the word "prayer" into a big red "button" inside me. Hearing (or reading) the word "prayer" punched my "button", sirens wailed, danger signs flashed inside my mind, and I'd be waved away from the whole concept by an internal "watchdog" figure — a cute bulldog-type cartoon figure with a big gold star on his chest like a Western sheriff. With the lights and sirens and barking dog, I found it pretty hard to settle down to pray.

As I understand it now, the "child-me" got the "watch-dog" to protect her, since her best efforts then were inadequate, and her experience of trying to pray were so sad and painful. Her "watchdog" had the job of listening for painful word associations, making very sure she got warned to stay away from them. He's been a loyal hardworking "watchdog". He cleverly installed "buttons" on several words which got associated at an early age when my vocabulary was small and my ability to think abstractly quite limited, with large areas of feelings or complicated patterns of events/behaviors. My "watchdog" was a survival mechanism, and a good one, too.

"Love", "needs", "leaving" and many other simple words as well as words like "bad", "God" or "pray" all had their "buttons" before ACoA, rooted in old associations made in childhood, associations the dictionary would not support, but which were real to me — painful, fearful, shocking and sad burdens of feelings and experiences. My definitions of these simple words were my best efforts as a child at comprehending a world I found myself in, a world largely out of control.

As I use the tools of the ACoA program to desensitize these overburdened and confused definitions, I can give my "watchdog" the task of sniffing out these old "buttons" and leading me to the experiences which tied these simple words to so much pain. I like to keep any allies that have been around since childhood as figures in my imagination. I find them to be sources of comfort, like the "watchdog". He was the child-me's protector, after all, so I let the adult-me scratch his ears!

Since visualization is a form of prayer I am especially comfortable with in recovery, I encourage myself in seeing the "watchdog". I let him see that we aren't in that old fearful world of childhood, that the "button" is just a false alarm here. This form of prayer is a way I see myself becoming unified, happy and whole with my past and present flowing together.

In recovery prayer has become a much freer exchange than I might have supposed. The dictionary tells me that "prayer" means "communication directed at God", including "asking, praising, adoring or confessing". I've come to see that I did a lot of praying when I was a child, but I didn't call it that because I thought praying meant begging or trying to make deals. But when I played in the soft green woods which surrounded my home, I adored and praised and asked — Nature, which is what I did accept.

As I've grown to accept a revised concept of God, one that includes personal love, life, diversity and joy, I've found it easier and easier to play at prayer, like in the case of getting to know my "watchdog". Instead of praying intellectually to have my unwillingness to pray removed, I let myself play at getting to know myself, letting my imagination have the freedom to lead me to a peaceful, unifying release.

This is a form of having faith that the Spiritual Power in me will guide me, heal me, restore me to wholeness. I'm sure that one way is as good as another, when it comes to prayer. It's just so much fun praying in pictures, stories, even in songs. As an ACoA, it is important for me to encourage myself in joy and humor.

I had thought that meditation was something difficult or complicated. I see now that I confused my peaceful times with daydreaming, discounting the inspiration and guidance that was always there for me. Once the confusion over these words, "prayer" and "meditation", is inventoried and replaced with realistic adult associations, I can begin building techniques and exploring various avenues in expanding both of these channels. I can also give myself credit for the ways I did pray and meditate, although I may not have called it that, as part of healing my self-concept, realizing that I am, and have always been, a child of a Loving Parent!

Where I notice that my prayers have been efforts to strike a "deal" with God, or to get God to do my will, I begin constructing new prayers — asking, praising, loving, admitting. Where I notice that my "meditations" have been on areas of worry, fear, obsession or anger, I use the steps to inventory those blocks to spiritual "tuning in". Where the habit of worry or other negative thinking is a factor, replacing those reflections with a visualization associated with God, as I understand God, is helpful.

I take myself on a "one-minute-vacation" to the seashore or the forest. Or I may allow myself to join my life with a rosebud, experience myself unfolding in fragrance on a summer morning. If I also get into the habit of taking a few slow, deep breaths as I do these visualizations, the old habits are gradually replaced. I've found that once I replaced one "rut" with a positive meditation, the process got much quicker and progressively easier to do — so long as I'm not trying to "stuff" or shut down issues that need inventory and the other steps.

I find that I spend more and more of my time experiencing some aspect of prayer and meditation. Worry, fear and other negative reactions like envy, insecurity *are* gradually being replaced with healthier activities.

### "First Things First!"

When other aspects of my life pull me into confusion, I remember to remind myself to take a deep breath, seek serenity, become heart-centered, establish conscious contact. Remembering to do this "First Things First" reaching out in prayer is the biggest change in me, since I've entered recovery/discovery.

Almost 12 years ago my good friend, Paul S. of Santa Cruz, taught me a prayer at my request. I was suicidal, broke, unable to take care of myself and I didn't want to die. I knew he and his wife Kai "did that sort of thing" — praying. We had known each other for years, and I wanted what they had: peace, joy, stability.

He taught me a simple prayer. It went, "Thank You, dear God, for the blessings of this day . . ." And then, I'd have to think of something I was grateful for, which wasn't so easy then, that's for sure! But I could admit to being grateful, that I wasn't in jail or stuck in a New York slum. (Both of these had been the case, too, so the gratitude was genuine.)

This simple prayer of praise, combined with the willingness to try it, began the process of my recovery. That gratitude prayer was my first introduction to a healthy communication with a God of generosity, not a deal-maker, harsh or unresponsive judge.

In the strange and wonderful way Life has of unfolding in recovery, Paul and Kai S. both have since joined the Twelve-Step process themselves, although it was several years later before the wheel turned that circle.

Step Eleven is a basic "First Things First" principle in ACoA. It's listed as "eleven", not "one" because the process of healing develops through the Steps, and I needed every one of them, Step by Step, to get me to a place inside myself where I admit that Step Eleven *is* central in my program of recovery. I needed to grow this far, using the Steps and the fellowship, so I can see that seeking conscious contact with the God of my understanding, seeking knowledge of God's will for me and the power to carry that out really *is* my primary goal in life and recovery.

## STEP TWELVE

# KEEP COMING BACK!
# *IT WORKS!*

---

*12. Having had a spiritual awakening as a result of these steps, we tried to carry this message to those who still suffer, and to practice these principles in all our affairs.*

---

If a "spiritual awakening" means sensing that this universe I'm in is a friendly one, a place where I am welcomed, nurtured and supported, then I've found this in ACoA. *Awakening to Spirit,* in my understanding, means experiencing a realization of Life as a totality in which I belong, have a personal role, an identity with meaning.

This sort of conception of "Spirit" needn't be conventionally religious from the point-of-view of an evolutionist. It's quite possible to feel this sort of unification simply by seeing myself as an expression of the species, just as welcomed and just as supported in my living as any other evolving life-form on this planet. This sort of view is much akin to the American Indian, Taoist and other Eastern understandings of Spirit, in which all life forms, along with the earth itself, the weather, time and history are held to be unified, inter-related, moving through a process so large we may not comprehend it, but in which we are entirely unquestionably joined — committed by the very fact of our existence to our role, identity and purpose in the process as a whole.

Of course, we remain entirely free in all of the Twelve-Step Programs to conceive of "Spirit" in any terms we like, traditional or not. God, as we understand God, is a basis upon which our ACoA program and fellowship establishes common ground, available to all who identify with the "Problem" and seek healing in the application of the "Solution" to their lives.

Becoming spiritually awakened, as a result of moving through the process of healing diagrammed by the Steps, amounts to acknowledgment that I am no longer alone in a world filled with people I can neither understand nor trust, vainly and blindly making the same unworkable attempts at getting out of my unhappy situation.

When I reflect back to the painful combination of uncertainty and need which dominated my awareness when I began recovery, and compare that to the ways I've changed my outlook and my behaviors as a result of these steps, it's easier to admit to "awakening". The simple action of attempting these steps — willingness to try combined with enough open-mindedness to face down my pre-conceived ideas about spiritual matters and the honesty it takes to look squarely at my situation — is in large part an antidote to isolation. Also undertaking the steps meant trying something new, breaking out of old routines, opening up alternative ways to look at old issues as well as entirely unsuspected avenues for exploration. I find that I am indeed moving out of isolation and breaking free of my old ruts of dysfunctional patterned behavior through this combination of insight to attempt healthy alternatives.

Tension, anxiety and the feeling of helplessness which had clouded my personal atmosphere before I began recovery are being replaced. Hopefulness, established as a result of experiencing progress, confidence to try, which is evidence of a growing self-esteem, are replacing the old discomforts as a result of these Steps and the support of fellowship in ACoA. Awakening to confidence, to hope, to the freedom to try in life, these are demonstrations of spiritual renewal, "a spiritual awakening", as I understand it.

I may not have all and everything I'd like in life right now, but I have certainly begun to move with life, toward hope and renewed possibility, and this is something I didn't have before ACoA.

ACoA's Twelve-Steps have offered me personal spiritual renewal — perhaps not the "bolt of lightning" preconceived idea I may have had of "spiritual awakening", but awakening nonetheless. I'll be content with a quieter sort of light, the hint of a rosy dawn in a sky that once seemed dark and hopeless to me. I'll let this light grow, little by little, in the happy realization that it will. This is very different than the fear I had, before ACoA and the Program of Twelve Steps, that there might not be a light for me!

# Carry The Message

Living this confidence and hope is a way I "carry the message" everywhere I go without making an extra effort to do so. It may well be true that this living demonstration is the strongest and most honest statement I can make. In "practicing these principles in all my affairs", I in turn *do* "carry the message".

The implied responsibility in Step Twelve, to ". . . carry this message to those who still suffer," requires some careful consideration, since we ACoAs are notorious "caretakers" in this world, inclined to take on roles of extra responsibility in other people's lives while avoiding dealing with ourselves. Better, I find, to concentrate on "practicing these principles" of healing my distorted self-concept, with its problems rooted deeply in my dysfunctional family experiences as a child, and allow applications of the "Solution" to dictate how and when I get involved with "carrying the message".

"The spiritual life is not a theory," page 83 of *The Big Book of Alcoholics Anonymous* states, (just a paragraph or two above the section widely quoted, the AA "Promises",) "You have to live it."

The natural desire most of us experience to "carry the message" when we've begun to realize the heartening results of our own attempts at this new way of life deserves expression, an expression which the Steps themselves inspire and direct, as I return again and again to seeking out ways these principles can come to life in and through me.

Because I know as a result of these Steps that I have a tendency to "take care of" others, to either seek control or to be self-manipulated by guilt, anger or fear of abandonment in my relationships, I remind myself of the principle, "Keep the focus on myself", contained in the "Solution". I also reaffirm to myself that ACoA "is a program of action coming from love" and that, in working the Steps on my resentments, fears and other negative emotions, I am clearing a channel in myself, permitting myself to experience this centering so that my own actions will be coming from love, not the reactions which are so indicative of my disorder.

By "keeping the focus on myself ", I take responsibility for making sure my needs are being met, rather than indulging in "wishful thinking" tendencies, such as kidding myself that my needs will "somehow" (magically?) be met if I take care of someone else and neglect my own responsibilities. By taking the commitment risks to expose my own goals and then putting in the work and sustained effort to move toward these, I demonstrate a real change from my former way of living.

The needs I'm challenged to take on in ACoA are those which remained unmet before beginning my recovery, needs like the need for intimacy, or fun, for better health practices or communications skills. By "keeping the focus on myself" in these important areas that brought me to recovery, I cease the old behaviors of concealing myself from myself. Hiding behind someone else, or creating crises, confusion, lack of focus in my life and affairs are gradually left behind.

These sorts of changes are bound to stir up interest in those who have known us. Opportunities to share my altered outlook and understanding with family members and friends arise without my necessarily bringing up the subject or "preaching ACoA". When "carrying the message" develops as a result of this "practicing the principles" in my relationships and affairs, the exchange is usually positive. There's no feeling of self-righteousness, of lecturing the other person, of taking the view that I'm making a judgment — calling the other person "sick", for example. It's vital, it seems to me, that I keep the focus of my ACoA program on me and my recovery, rather than to fall into the trap of using ACoA as a shield of righteousness in a crusade of self-justification. This tendency toward control or intimidation is a weakness which can quickly cloud my sight or lose me in self-imposed isolation!

If "action coming from love" is action, not reaction, in the meaning indicated in the "Problem" and the "Solution", then I must continue to apply the Steps to my responses, examining my motives to clear away resentment, fear, or concealed desires to manipulate, since failing to keep up this practice can lead to self-deception. This goal of "action, not reaction" is a keystone in the structure we are building for ourselves to make sure to the best of my ability today that I am acting, not reacting. I become freed, little by little, from old habitual reactions which more or less controlled my life before ACoA.

The fear that I might not be lovable or attractive, for example, may have led me in the past to attempt to manipulate those I loved. Or perhaps I habitually jumped to conclusions and didn't let others get out their ideas or communicate to me because I had a "know it all" attitude about certain topics, or was insecure about my ability to win an argument. Maybe the desire to be important or respected led me to exaggerate or to create impressions I later couldn't sustain. These are all forms of habitual reaction which "action coming from love" would modify, dictating real changes, noticable to others as well as to myself.

In my grateful commitment to "carry the message to those who still suffer", it's important that I do all that I can to make sure that I'm not concealing "people-pleasing — people-controlling" habits and mixing up the "message" with old manipulations. Besides looking myself in the eye in the mirror every morning becomes a friendlier and friendlier prospect, the more I'm personally centered in "action coming from love" in all of my affairs.

## Keep Coming Back. *It Works!*

In ACoA rotation of leadership, the give and take of the sponsorship relationship, and the continuing unfolding of each of our individual recoveries softens the impact of any individual's personality, rounding out and balancing "the message" to the newcomers. The slogan, "Keep Coming Back! *It Works!*" assures us that whatever our biases, shortcomings or lapses, this recovery we have begun in ACoA continues to welcome each and every one of us, no matter what. I do my best, one day at a time, to "practice these principles", and to let that practice dictate and mold the ways I "carry the message", but I bear in mind that "Keep Coming Back!" is meant for *me*, and not just for the newcomer. I'm not through yet with the process of recovery/discovery. There's more to come.

"Keep Coming Back! *It Works!*" is a kind of cheerful admonishment to keep a fresh approach, an open mind *and* heart to what blessings are yet undiscovered, still to emerge or be created. It was such a friendly thing to hear, when I was new and so afraid I wouldn't be accepted at the meetings: "Keep Coming Back!" you said, and I *did*!

I still continue to "Keep Coming Back!", but I don't do it to do someone else a favor. I do it because I'm not finished yet with my own growth and recovery.

Occasionally an idea that I don't need ACoA anymore, that I've outgrown it or have recovered somehow to a point where I no longer require meetings comes into my mind. When I notice this sort of thinking, I look on it as an indication that my tendency to withdraw into isolation may be reasserting itself, and I check out my life and affairs to see if there is something I am inclined to avoid or to stuff. Or is someone in the fellowship reminding me of issues rooted in my childhood, pushing my "button" about something I need to inventory but still fear?

Fortunately, ACoA will always welcome me again if I do pull back on my own for a time for one reason or another. We don't make judgments or rules for other people in ACoA. Instead we keep the focus on ourselves, and we "Keep Coming Back!" We do this *because "It Works!" for us,* in our own continuing recoveries and not as "caretaking" or "people pleasing".

"Keep Coming Back! *It Works!*" is something I say because it's true for me in my life. When I heard you say this, back when I was new to meetings and to the possibility of ACoAs recovery in my life, you inspired me with hope, because you were telling me *the truth* about your own experience. It has become a living reality for me now, too. Thanks to all of *you* who've shared your experience, strength and hope with me.

Thank *you* for being there!

And please "KEEP COMING BACK! *IT WORKS!*"

## THE MAGAZINE FOR AND ABOUT . . .

# ADULT CHILDREN OF ALCOHOLICS

## WE UNDERSTAND. . .

. . . what it means to be the child of an alcoholic. We know the confusion, the intense self-criticism, the bottled-up anger you carry with you. You are not alone.

How do we know? Because we, like you, are part of the 28 million Americans who are children of alcoholics. And we have seen our numbers grow into a social movement focused on the special needs and understanding of people like us.

*Changes* . . . The Magazine For and About Children of Alcoholics, is part of the new vision of hope for CoAs everywhere. The understanding that comes from caring can lead to healing. But none of us can do it alone. We need each other. The isolation, desolation and despair of the alcoholic family is not all that binds us. It is the hope — and the truth — that things will get better.

We hope you share in the vision by subscribing to *Changes* . . . For and About Children of Alcoholics. It's a change for the better.

_____

☐ **YES** . . . Send my subscription to the following address:
☐ 1 Year (6 Issues) . . . $18.00     ☐ 2 Years (12 Issues) . . . $34.00

**Your Name:** _____

**Address:** _____

_____/_____

Payment Form (Check One):

☐ Check or Money Order Enclosed (Payable to The U.S. Journal)

☐ M.C. #: _____ Exp. Date: _____

☐ VISA #: _____ Exp. Date: _____

Agency P.O.'s & Vouchers accepted. Attach documentation for billing purposes.

**Cardholder's Signature:** _____

### The U.S. Journal, Inc., 3201 S.W. 15th Street, Enterprise Center
### Deerfield Beach, FL 33442 • 1-800-851-9100